Barcelona

Spain

EVERYMAN
CITY GUIDES

EVERYMAN CITY GUIDES
Copyright © 2000 David
Campbell Publishers, London

ISBN 1-85715-619-6

First published April 2000

Originally published in
France by Nouveaux Loisirs,
a subsidiary of Gallimard,
Paris 1999, and in Italy by
Touring Editore, Srl.,
Milano 1999.

Copyright © 1999
Nouveaux Loisirs,
Touring Editore, Srl.

SERIES EDITORS
Seymourina Cruse and
Marisa Bassi
BARCELONA EDITION:
Ædelsa Atelier Tourisme
GRAPHICS
Élizabeth Cohat, Yann Le Duc
LAYOUT:
Silvia Pecora
MINI-MAPS:
Fiammetta and Flavio Badalato
MAPS OF THE AREA:
Édigraphie
STREET MAPS:
Touring Club Italiano
PRODUCTION
Catherine Bourrabier

Translated by Matthew Clarke
and typeset by The Write Idea
in association with
First Edition Translations Ltd,
Cambridge, UK

Printed in Italy by
Editoriale Lloyd

Authors
BARCELONA

Getting there : Marta Sardá (1)
A journalist with the Catalan daily paper
Avui, she is an inquisitive and indefatigable
traveler. She has worked on many Catalan,
Spanish and Italian publications.

Where to stay and **Where to
eat:** Enric Marín (2)
In his professional life he combines the
knowledge accredited by a degree in the
History of Art with family tradition – his
uncles still run a hotel in the Balearic
Islands. An expert in Spanish regional
cooking, he has a weakness for Catalan
gastronomy and hotels with charm.

After dark: Margarita Puig (3)
After graduating in Information Science at
the Autonomous University of Barcelona,
she worked as a journalist on the *Diario de
Barcelona* and took part in several programs
for Catalan television. She writes two
columns for the daily paper *La Vanguardia*:
'Suggestion of the day …' and, on Mondays,
'Contra', together with Marius Carol.

What to see and **Further afield:**
Miquel Villagrasa (4)
Born in 1951 in the historical heart of
Barcelona, which he has never left, he is the
editor of *La Vanguardia*, the prestigious daily
newspaper dating back to 1881. A professor
for more than ten years in the Faculty of
Communication Science of the Autonomous
University of Barcelona, he devotes his free
time to the study and improvement of the
most typical spots in his home town.

Where to shop: Óscar Muñoz (5)
A regular contributor to the daily
newspaper *La Vanguardia*, he knows the city
like the back of his hand, and specializes in
information on leisure and tourism. One of
his greatest joys is exploring the *carrers* and
avingudes of Barcelona in search of new
haunts: stores, galleries, bookstores … The
journalist Jordi Ortiz Lombardía has also
contributed to this part of the guide.

*Note from the publisher:
To keep the price of this guide as low as
possible we decided on a common edition for
the UK and US, which has meant
American spelling.*

Key

The Insider's Guide is made up of **8 sections** each indicated by a different color.

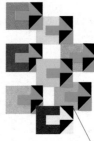

Things you need to know (mauve)
Where to stay (blue)
Where to eat (red)
After dark (pink)
What to see (green)
Further afield (orange)
Where to shop (yellow)
Finding your way (purpl

🚌 61 🕐 Apr.–under-18s ♿

Practical information is given for each particular establishment: opening times, prices, ways of paying, different services available

How to use this guide

In the area

In 1929 the Montjuïc hill was chosen
Exhibition: major buildings were put

Romanesque art secti
collection of medieval

The section
"In the area"
refers you (➡ 00) to
other establishments
that are covered in a
different section of the
guide but found in the
same area of the city.

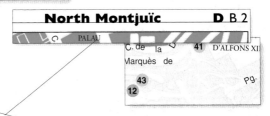

North Montjuïc   **D** B 2

PALAU

C. de la   **41**   D'ALFONS XI
Marquès de

43
12

Pg.

The small map
shows all the
establishments
mentioned and others
described elsewhere but
found "in the area", by the
color of the section.

**The name of the
district** is given above
the map. A grid reference
(**A** B-C 2) enables you to
find it in the section on
Maps at the end of the
book.

"Good value!"
The star sign indicates modestly
priced hotels and restaurants.

Not forgetting

■ **Poble Espanyol (43)** Avinguda
☎ 93 325 78 66 🕐 Mon. 9am–8pm; T

The section "Not forgetting"
lists other useful addresses in the same area.

The opening page
to each section contains
an index ordered
alphabetically (Getting
there), by subject or by
district (After dark) as
well as useful addresses
and advice.

**The section
"Things you need
to know"** covers
information on getting

to Barcelona and day-
to-day life in the city.

Theme pages
introduce a selection
of establishments on
a given topic.

**The "Maps"
section** of this guide
contains 6 street plans
of Barcelona followed
by a detailed index.

Spanish Tourist Office in the UK, 23
Manchester Square, London W1 ☎ (020)
7486 8077; 0901 669920 **Spanish Tourist
Office in the USA**, 666 Fifth Avenue
(35th Floor), New York, NY 10103
☎ 212-265 8822 ➡ 212-265 8864
@ www.bcn.es (in English)

Getting there

Catalan and Spanish

Catalan is spoken in Barcelona; this
is not a dialect of Spanish, but a
language in its own right. Although
the Catalans are completely
bilingual, they nevertheless prefer
to express themselves in their own
language, which is used for the
names of streets and subway
stations and all signposts. However,
information on the signs inside train
and subway stations is also written
in Spanish.

Electric current

This is supplied at 220 volts, using two-pin plugs, as in the rest of Europe (apart from Great Britain). An adaptor is therefore required to use electrical appliances with three pins.

Things you need to know

Tourist information

Pl. Catalunya, 17 underground (near Av. Portal de l'Àngel)
☎ 90 630 12 82 / 93 304 34 21 *(international customers)* /
93 304 32 32 *(hotel service)*
🕓 *daily 9am–9pm (closed on Christmas Day and New Year's Day)*
Ⓜ *Catalunya*
Barcelona Sants train station (in the main hall)
☎ 93 491 44 31
🕓 *Mon.–Fri. 8am–8pm; Sat., Sun., public holidays 8am–2pm*
Ⓜ *Sants Estació*
Pl. Sant Jaume (ground floor of the Ajuntament, the City Hall)
🕓 *Mon.–Sat. 10am–8pm; Sun., public holidays 10am–2pm*
Ⓜ *Jaume I*

INDEX A–Z

Basic facts

The Spanish airline Iberia offers daily direct flights to Barcelona from New York, and also flights via Madrid from Miami and Los Angeles; both Iberia and British Airways have daily flights from London and Manchester. The Barcelona-El Prat airport is 8 miles from the city center, but a new

Getting there

AEROBUS

Information

General
In the arrival area of Terminal A
☎ 93 298 38 38
➡ 93 298 37 37
🕒 24 hr

Tourist Office
Terminal A
☎ 93 478 47 04
🕒 Mon.–Sat.
9.30am–3pm
Terminal B
☎ 93 478 05 65
🕒 Mon.–Sat.
9.30am–8pm; Sun., public holidays
9.30am–3pm; closed January 1, Good Friday, May 1, September 11, December 24 and 25.

Lost property
Between terminals B and C
☎ 93 298 38 38
🕒 24 hr

Police
Outside Terminal A
☎ 93 298 33 54
🕒 24 hr

Left luggage
Terminal B
☎ 93 298 38 38
🕒 24 hr
● 635 Ptas per day

Airlines

Iberia
In the airport:
Terminal B
☎ 90 240 05 00
🕒 24 hr
In the city: Plaça

de Espanya, 1
☎ 93 325 73 58
🕒 Mon.–Fri.
9am–6pm
Carrer Diputació, 258
☎ 93 401 33 96
🕒 Mon.–Fri.
9am–6pm

British Airways
In the airport:
Terminal A
☎ 93 298 33 99
🕒 daily
6am–6.30pm
In the city: Passeig de Gràcia, 16
☎ 90 213 21 32

Getting into the city

Train
This is the

quickest way of reaching the city center. The airport's train station is next to terminal A, and there is access to it via a moving walkway. 2 stops before Barcelona: El Prat de Llobregat and Bellvitge; 4 stops in Barcelona: Estació de Sants, Plaça de Catalunya, Arc de Triomf and Clot. Reckon on 20 mins for Estació de Sants. Buy your ticket before boarding the train.

🕒 departure from

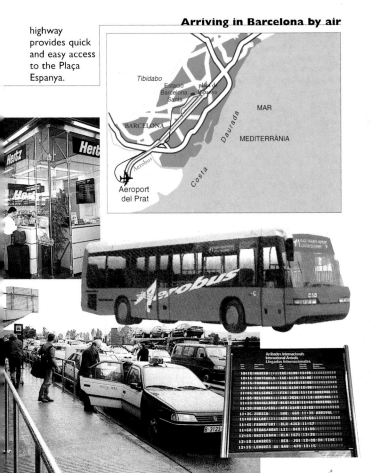

highway provides quick and easy access to the Plaça Espanya.

the airport: Mon.–Fri. 6.13am–10.41pm every 30 mins; Sat., Sun. 5.43am–10.13pm every 30 mins Departure from the city center: Mon.–Fri. 5.43am–10.13pm every 30 mins; Sat., Sun. 5.46am–10.17pm every 30 mins
● Mon.–Fri. 305 Ptas; Sat., Sun. 350 Ptas

Aerobus

Three stops in the airport: terminals A, B and Pont Aeri. Departure every 15 mins. Stops heading to the

city center: Plaça Espanya; Gran Via/Urgell; Universitat; Plaça de Catalunya. Stops heading to the airport: Diputació/Passeig de Gràcia; Roma/Urgell; Estació de Sants; Plaça Espanya. Reckon on around 60 mins for the journey.
🔵 from the airport: Mon.–Fri. 6.30am–11pm; Sat., Sun., public holidays 6.30am–10.50pm
🔵 from the city center: Mon.–Fri. 5.30am–10.05pm; Sat., Sun., public

holidays 6am–10.20pm
● one way 475 Ptas; round trip 950 Ptas 1,900 Ptas (ticket valid for 3 days on all public transport) 2,400 Ptas (ticket valid for 5 days on all public transport)

Taxis

Taxi stands in front of terminals A, B and Pont Aeri. Reckon on a journey of 50 mins to the Plaça de Catalunya. Pay in cash, and top up with a tip.
● 2,500 Ptas to the Plaça de Catalunya in normal traffic conditions.

(Supplements: suitcase 100 Ptas, animal 125 Ptas, airport tax 300 Ptas).
Cars equipped for the disabled on request
☎ 934208088

Foreign exchange

In the arrival areas of terminals A and B
🔵 7am–11pm

Car rental

Avis and Hertz counters in all the terminals
Avis
☎ 93 478 17 00
Hertz
☎ 93 836 37 19

9

Basic facts

Although romantics may choose to arrive by boat — there is a ferry service linking Barcelona with the Balearic Islands — more mundane means of transport are the train — the Talgo Joan Miró leaves every night from Paris-Austerlitz; the car, through France — the French border is only some

▶Getting there

Train

To reach Barcelona by train from London, it is necessary to change in Paris and catch an overnight train from Austerlitz station. The journey takes about 24 hours and ends in the Estació de Sants.

Estació de Sants

This is Barcelona's main train station, for international and long-distance Spanish routes and it has links with the airport. The station is served by the subway lines 3 and 5 and by various city and regional buses.

Booking information
☎ 93 495 62 15 / 495 60 37 / 491 25 86
🕐 daily
7.30am–10.30pm

Left luggage
🕐 daily
6.30am–11pm

Estació de França

Regional trains and trains from other parts of Spain stop here. Situated near the port, it was once the city's main station. The Barceloneta subway station (line 4) is nearby.

Booking information
☎ 93 496 34 64
🕐 daily

7.30am–10.30pm

Left luggage
🕐 daily
6.30am–11pm

Car

By road and motorway

Catalonia has an extensive network of motorways, which usually require a toll charge. From La Jonquera (on the French border) take the A7 right up to Barcelona.
● from La Jonquera to Barcelona 1,200 Ptas.
It is also possible, though not advisable, to take the national road (N11): the journey will take three times as

long! Barcelona is flanked by two ring roads (the Ronda del Litoral, on the coast, and the Ronda de Dalt, in the hills). The A19 *autopista* — motorway — from Maresme connects Barcelona with the Costa Brava, while the highway to Castelldefels provides a link to the coastal region of Garraf. Both these areas are very popular with Barcelona residents on weekends and during the holiday season.

Regulations

US and EC driving licenses are

100 miles away; and the long-distance bus, the cheapest option.

recognized; if you are driving your own car, you must have a green card from your insurance company.
Speed limit on motorways: 120 km/hr (75 miles/hr). Spanish law punishes drunken driving very severely. It is therefore imperative to drink only in moderation.

Gas
The price of gas can vary from one gas station to the next: unleaded gas costs around 125 Ptas/liter, and diesel around 89 Ptas/liter.

Information and emergencies
Mossos d'Esquadra (Catalan police)
☎ 93 300 22 96
for emergencies:
☎ 93 300 91 91
Prefectura Provincial de Trànsit
☎ 90 012 35 05
Autopistes de Catalunya (Catalan motorways)
☎ 93 228 50 00
Autopistes d'Espanya (Spanish motorways)
☎ 93 228 50 00

Long-distance bus
The Estació d'Autobusos

Barcelona Nord, better known as the Estació del Nord (Carrer Ali-Bei, 80) is Barcelona's main long-distance bus station.
☎ 93 265 65 08
Ⓜ *Arc de Triomf (15 mins on foot, but it is a better idea to take a taxi if you are carrying luggage)*
● *no more than 1,000 Ptas, in normal traffic conditions*

Left luggage
☎ 93 265 65 08
Ⓞ *daily 5.30am–1am*

Boat
A great many cruisers call at Barcelona, and

there are ferries which leave regularly for the Balearic Islands and Genoa.
☎ 93 263 36 00
Estació Marítima Balears
Moll Sant Bertran, 3
☎ 93 295 91 00
Left luggage
Ⓞ *daily 9am– 1pm, 4–11pm*
Estació Marítima Internacional
Moll Barcelona, 1
☎ 93 221 83 15
/ 93 221 83 67
Left luggage
Ⓞ *daily 8am–3pm*
Companyia Trans-mediterrània
Moll Sant Bertran, 3
☎ 90 245 46 45
/ 93 295 91 00

Basic facts

Although the subway, with 5 lines serving most of Barcelona's neighborhoods, is the most practical means of transport, the buses (78 routes) undoubtedly constitute the most enjoyable way of getting around town – Subway line 1 has the best facilities for the disabled. The subway stations can be

Getting around

Subway

5 lines with 111 stations cross the city. 88% of the network is equipped with air-conditioning – particularly welcome in summer. Each line has its own color: L1 red; L2 purple; L3 green; L4 yellow; L5 blue.
☼ *Mon.–Thu. 5am–11pm; Fri., Sat., day before public holidays 5am–2am; Sun. 6am–midnight; mid-week public holidays 6am–11pm; other public holidays 6am–2am*
● *145 Ptas; T-1 ticket, valid for 10 journeys on the subway or bus, 795 Ptas*

Bus

800 buses, on 78 routes, serve the whole of Barcelona, carrying more than 200 million passengers every year.
● *145 Ptas; T-1 ticket, valid for 10 journeys on the subway or bus, 795 Ptas*

Taxis

Around 8,000 yellow and black taxis serve Barcelona. Even though there are many taxi stands in the city, especially at tourist spots (the airport, train and bus stations, shopping malls and major thoroughfares),

they can also be hailed in the street. They are free when the green light on the roof is switched on.
● *300 Ptas basic rate, plus 110 Ptas/ km on weekdays from 6am to 10pm, or 120 Ptas/km on Sat., Sun. and at nights from 10pm to 6am*

Information, complaints, lost property
☎ 93 481 00 85
Radiotaxi
Miramar
☎ 93 433 10 20
Móvil, S.A.
☎ 93 358 11 11

Car

The city's traffic system is very simple, especially in the Eixample neighborhood,

with its regular checkerboard layout. With a few exceptions, the streets here are one-way and run in alternate directions: vertically, one street goes toward the sea, the next toward the hills; horizontally, one goes to the right, the next to the left. Barcelona has a large number of underground parking lots and several 'blue zones', or areas where you must pay to park. Do not leave any valuable objects inside your car. There are also many pedestrian or semi-pedestrian areas. In the old

distinguished by an 'M' on a diamond-shaped sign.

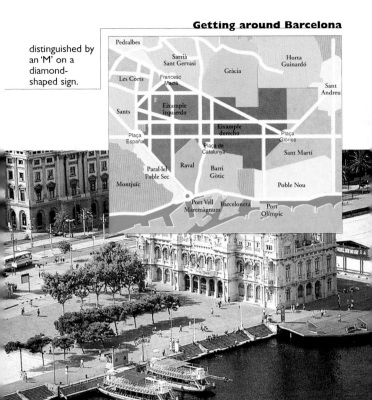

town, the Avinguda Portal de l'Àngel and the adjacent streets are only for pedestrians Mon.–Sat. 11am–2pm and 5pm–8pm; Sun. 5pm–8pm, and Carrer Ferran is closed to traffic every day from 11am to 3pm and 5pm to 8pm.

Tourist rides

Bus Turístic
24 stops at tourist spots.
◯ *Mar. 28–Jan. 6: daily, first departure from the Plaça Catalunya at 9am*
● *1,700 Ptas for one day; 2,300 Ptas for two days*

Tranvia Blau
From the Plaça Kennedy to the cable-car railroad leading to the Tibidabo funfair.
☎ *93 298 70 00/ 93 318 69 27*

Tibibús
From the Plaça Catalunya to the Plaça Tibidabo.
◯ *Sat., Sun., public holidays; in summer, from June 23, Tue.– Sun., first departure from the Plaça Catalunya at 11am; last departure from Tibidabo, 30 mins before funfair closes. Every 30 mins (on the hour and the half-hour) on weekends and on public holidays; every hour on weekdays.*

Golondrines
These tourist boats ply around the harbor from the Port Vell to the Escullera.
☎ *93 442 31 06*
◯ *daily; the timetable varies according to the season*

Trimar
A catamaran which links the Moll de Colom with the Bogatell beach.
◯ *July, Aug.: Mon.–Fri. 11.30am, 1.15pm, 4.30pm, 6.15pm; Sat., Sun., public holidays 11.30am, 1.15pm, 4.30pm, 6.15pm, 8.15pm*
The timetable varies according to the weather.

Horse-drawn carriages
At the Portal de la Pau (at the bottom of the Rambla) for an original trip around town.
☎ *93 421 88 04*

Tren Montjuïc
Small two-coach train (58 people max.) which goes up the hill.
☎ *93 415 60 20*
◯ *during Easter week and June 22–Sep. 13, every 30 mins. Departure: Plaça Espanya.*
Route: Pl. Espanya, Pavelló de Mies van der Rohe, Poble Espanyol, Museu Nacional d'Art de Catalunya, Jardins Joan Maragall, Piscines Picornell, Galeria Olímpica, Castell de Montjuïc (Museu Militar), Mirador de l'Alcalde, Fundació Joan Miró, Museu Etnològic, Museu Arqueológic, pl. de Espanya

Basic facts

At night Barcelona does not shut down: night owls can find a well-stocked supermarket, open until the early hours, at number 7 on the Rambla de Catalunya, as well as newspaper kiosks open round the clock, also on the Ramblas. The city's main services have telephones which are

➡ Getting by

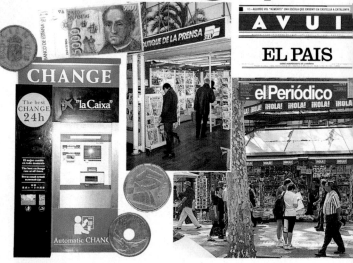

Consulates

United States Consulate
Pg. Reina Elisenda Montcada, 23
☎ 93 280 02 95
British Consulate
Avenida Diagonal, 477
☎ 93 419 90 44

Money

The currency in Spain is the Peseta.
100 Ptas = approx. 40p (UK); 60 cents (US)
1 Euro = 166 Ptas
Coins of 1, 5, 10, 25, 50, 100, 200 and 500 Ptas; bills of 1,000, 2,000, 5,000 and 10,000 Ptas.

Foreign exchange

Cash or travelers' checks can be changed in any bank, on presentation of identity documents.
🕐 Mon.-Fri. 8am-12pm; Sat. 8am-12pm
The savings banks (caixas) close on Saturdays, but open on Thursday afternoons. Most have automatic cashpoints for credit cards.

Lost credit cards

Visa-Master Card
☎ 93 315 25 12 / 91 519 21 00
American Express
☎ 91 572 03 20 / 91 570 77 77
Diner's Club
☎ 915474000

Tipping

Service is always included, but a tip is appreciated (100 Ptas minimum), even in simple restaurants.

With taxi drivers, reckon on 10% of the total charge.

Media

International press

Foreign newspapers and magazines are easy to find in the kiosks in the center, especially on the Rambla (**1**) and the Passeig de Gràcia (**2**).

Spanish press

Catalan dailies:
Avui and El Periódico de Catalunya
Spanish dailies:
El País, El Periódico de Catalunya (Spanish edition), La Vanguardia, El Mundo Catalunya
Weekly:
Guía del Ocio, the indispensable leisure guide for Barcelona

(restaurants, museums, exhibitions, shows and concerts).

Television

Main channels in Catalan:
TV3, C33 and Barcelona Televisió, exclusively devoted to the city.
Channels in Spanish:
TV1 and TV2, Antena 3 TV, Tele 5 and Canal Plus (cable channel), although regional programmes are in Catalan.

Radio

Catalunya Radio and Catalunya Informació both broadcast entirely in Catalan, the former being especially popular. There are many other stations which broadcast in both languages, manned 24 hours a day, and the City Hall information service can be reached at any time by dialing 010.

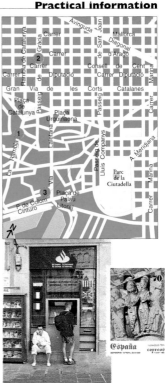

in particular *RNE*, *Ser* and *Onda Cero.*

Telephones

Prefixes
In Spain the provincial prefixes are an integral part of the number. In Barcelona this is 93.

Phoning Barcelona:
Barcelona:
00 + 34 + number
Phoning the US:
00 + 1 + number
Phoning the UK:
00 + 44 + number

Public telephones
These take coins or phonecards (1,000 and 2,000 Ptas), available in tobacconists (*estanques*), department stores and newsagents. The first unit costs

25 Ptas.

Useful numbers
National information
☎ *1003*
International information
☎ *025*
Collect calls
☎ *1009*

Mail

Central post office (4)
pl. Antonio López, 1
Ⓜ *Jaume I*
☎ *90 219 71 97*
🕒 *Mon.–Fri. 9am–9pm; Sat. 9am–1pm*

Other post offices
🕒 *Mon.–Fri. 8.30am–8.30pm; Sat. 9am–2pm*

Telegrams
☎ *93 322 20 00*
🕒 *daily, 24 hr*

Postal rates
For a postcard or normal letter,

70 Ptas to Europe and 115 Ptas to the US. Stamps are sold in post offices and tobacconists.

Mailboxes
These are well distributed throughout Barcelona: yellow ones for normal mail, red ones for urgent deliveries.

Emergencies

Health emergencies and ambulances
☎ *061*

Late-night pharmacies
☎ *93 481 00 60*

Fire service
☎ *080*

Police
☎ *091*

Hospitals
EU citizens can receive free treatment in the

state hospitals listed below, if they carry an E111 form, obtainable from their local social security office. Other visitors should have medical insurance.
Hospital General de la Vall d'Hebron
☎ *93 274 61 00*
Hospital Clínic i Provincial
☎ *93 227 54 00*
Hospital de la Santa Creu i Sant Pau
☎ *93 291 91 91*
Hospital Sant Joan Deu
☎ *93 280 40 00*

Lost property
Carrer Ciutat, 9
☎ *93 317 38 79*
🕒 *Mon.–Fri. 9am–2pm*

◆ **Where to stay**

Cheap solutions

It is still possible to stay in Barcelona on a modest budget. Youth hostels belonging to the IYHF offer the best guarantee of quality, though in the high season you will only be able to stay for three nights.

Alberg Palau *Pla de Palau, 6 - 08002* ☎ *93 412 50 80* Ⓜ *Jaume I*
Kabul *Plaça Reial, 17 - 08002* ☎ *93 318 51 90* Ⓜ *Liceu*
IYHF youth hostels
Alberg Internacional 2 *Passeig de Colom, 3 - 08002* ☎ *93 318 06 31*
Ⓜ *Drassanes*
Alberg Pere Tarrés *Carrer Numància, 149 - 08029* ☎ *93 410 23 09*
Ⓜ *Les Corts*

Be warned: book ahead

In the last ten years the tourist industry in Barcelona has mushroomed, and this has led to the construction of a large number of hotels. Nevertheless, in high season (Easter, August, New Year) you will not find a bed in Barcelona if you have not taken the precaution of booking ahead!
Central reservation ☎ 93 304 32 32

36
Hotels

THE INSIDER'S FAVORITES

How to read our selection

The selected hotels are classified on the basis of five price ranges, which reflect the cost of a double room, including tax and breakfast. The main services offered by the hotel are also indicated (see the list of pictograms on page 5). The breakfast symbol means that this meal can be provided by room service.

In the area

The Barri Gòtic, the oldest part of the city, was the site chosen by the Romans, in the reign of Augustus, to found their new colony. Ever since then the neighborhood has always provided the seats of government for Barcelona. It also houses the cathedral and the palace where the

Where to stay

Hotel Colón (1)
Avinguda Catedral, 7 - 08002 ☎ 93 301 14 04 ➡ 93 317 29 15

Ⓜ *Jaume I* *138 rooms* (9 suites) ●●● ▢ ▣ ▤ ▥ ▦ safe ▧ ▨ ▩ ▪ ▫
@ colon@nexus.es

Situated directly opposite the cathedral ➡ 86, this splendid building, with its air of an English cottage, undoubtedly boasts the best location in town, as it provides an unbeatable view of the sanctuary … especially on Sundays at noon, when the cathedral square plays host to the traditional *sardanes* – the rings of dancers can be appreciated even better from above! The cozy rooms – be sure to choose one on the top floor with a terrace overlooking the cathedral – the restful atmosphere and the attentive service all add to its charm. The only blot on the copybook: the hotel does not have any parking space, although the cathedral's underground parking lot is not far away.

Gran Hotel Barcino (2)
Carrer Jaume I, 6 - 08002 ☎ 93 302 20 12 ➡ 93 301 42 42

Ⓜ *Jaume I* *53 rooms* (3 suites) ●●● ▢ ▣ ▤ ▥ ▦ safe ▧ *buffet* ▨

This practical and elegant hotel, which was opened in 1996, has opted for a state-of-the-art look in its comfortable rooms, some of which even have bathrooms fitted out with a jacuzzi. However, it has no restaurant or conference rooms … and the nearest parking lot is over 200 yards away.

Hotel Rialto (3)
Carrer Ferran, 42 - 08002 ☎ 93 318 52 12 ➡ 93 318 53 12

Ⓜ *Jaume I* *162 rooms* ●● ▢ ▤ ▥ ▦ safe ▧ ▨ *buffet*

A highly successful restoration project has transformed the birthplace of the painter Joan Miró by highlighting the beams and exposing the stonework in the public areas. The rooms have been soundproofed. Do not miss the collection of fossils on show in the rooms given over to breakfast and buffets. The hotel's location, between the Rambla and the Plaça Sant Jaume, is a great asset.

Hotel Suizo (4)
Plaça del Àngel, 12 - 08002 ☎ 93 310 61 08 ➡ 93 315 04 61

Ⓜ *Jaume I* *50 rooms* ●● ▢ ▣ ▤ ▥ ▦ safe ▧ ▨ ▩ *buffet* ▪

Housed in a beautiful building on the site of the old Roman prison, the Hotel Suizo dominates the Plaça del Àngel and has the advantage of being right in front of the subway station. Ask for rooms on the upper floors looking outward, as the square is pretty lively! The restaurant serves Mediterranean and continental cuisine.

Not forgetting

■ **Hotel Gótico (5)** Carrer Jaume I, 14 - 08002 ☎ 93 315 22 11 ➡ 93 310 40 81 ●● *An old hotel which has been refurbished. The rooms are simple but comfortable. No parking lot or restaurant.*
■ **Hotel Residencia Colón (6)** Carrer Sagristans, 13/17 - 08002 ☎ 93 318 98 58 ➡ 93 317 28 22 ●● *Less expensive than the Colón, but it also offers friendly service, comfortable rooms and a view of the cathedral …*

Castilian king and queen welcomed Christopher Columbus on his return from America in 1492.

Breakfast at Barcelona's hotels is excellent; you will enjoy generous helpings and pleasant and efficient service.

In the area

This famous avenue, flanked by plane trees, buzzing at every hour of the day and night with a colorful motley throng, is obviously one of the city's main centers of attraction. A good show is always guaranteed: mimes, musicians, living statues and fortune-tellers entertain the gaping

Where to stay

Hotel Le Méridien (7)
La Rambla, 111 - 08002 ☎ 93 318 62 00 ➡ 93 301 77 76

Ⓜ *Catalunya* Ⓟ 🅗 *208 rooms (4 suites)* ●●●● ▨ ▣ ☎ Ⅲ ⌘ *"Le Patio"*
(Mediterranean cooking) 🅨 ♦ *adapted rooms* ✸

Ever since it opened in the 1950s this hotel has been a favorite with performing artists, particularly the big stars of the opera world appearing at the Teatre del Liceu ➡ 66, actors and rock stars – Michael Jackson stays there when he is in town … The 1930s-style rooms, complete with huge beds and bathrooms, are spacious and comfortable. The service is top rank. Non-smokers and business people have not been forgotten: the former have one floor to themselves, the latter have access to a business center!

Hotel Rivoli (8)
La Rambla, 118 - 08002 ☎ 93 302 66 43 ➡ 93 317 20 38

Ⓜ *Catalunya 81 rooms (9 suites)* ●●●● ▨ ▣ ☎ ▯ Ⅲ *safe* ⌘ 🅨 ⍟ ✸
terrace ♦ ✸ ⌸ ✗ *sauna, solarium* @ *rivoli@alba.mssl.es*

The attractively renovated Rivoli harmoniously combines classical, Art Deco and modern elements: the entrance hall with trompe-l'œil decorations, the dining-room lined with paintings, the bedrooms – enormous, comfortable and soundproofed, with their 1930s-style furniture and pastel tones. Its terrace affords an unmatched view of the city's historic center. The conference rooms are equipped to receive computers, microphones, television, telephones and fax. The hotel has its own internal television channel.

Hotel Ambassador (9)
Carrer Pintor Fortuny, 13 - 08001 ☎ 93 412 05 30 ➡ 93 317 20 38

Ⓜ *Catalunya* Ⓟ *96 rooms (9 suites)* ●●●● ▨ ▣ ☎ ▯ Ⅲ *safe* ⌘ 🅨 ✸
terrace ♦ ✸ ⌸ ✗ *sauna, solarium* ⍢ @ *rivoli@alba.mssl.es*

'A beautiful beginning' declare the owners, recalling the hotel's opening for the Olympic Games in 1992. Their first guests were indeed memorable: the prestigious 'Dream Team', the American basketball team which truly did make spectators dream. The spacious rooms flaunt the most up-to-date design. The Ambassador has provided business people with several rooms for conferences and meetings, equipped with all the necessary installations. A beautiful open air swimming pool makes it possible to sunbathe or take a dip … in the heart of the city. Following the lead of the Rivoli, it has its own internal television channel.

Not forgetting

■ **Hotel España (10)** Carrer Sant Pau, 9 - 08001 ☎ 93 318 17 58
➡ 93 317 11 34 ● *Built by Domènech i Muntaner, the España has seen better days, but the Modernist décor on the ground floor is worth a visit, if only to have breakfast!* ■ **Hotel Oriente (11)** - Rambla, 45/47 - 08002 ☎ 93 302 25 58
➡ 93 412 38 19 ●●● *This hotel, which opened in 1842, proudly declares itself to be the oldest hotel in Barcelona. Unfortunately, the service leaves a lot to be desired.*
■ **Hotel Peninsular (12)** C. Sant Pau, 34 - 08001 ☎ 93 302 31 38
➡ 93 412 36 99 ● *For fans of Modernism in search of somewhere cheap and central.*

onlookers, and the hospitable terraces of the string of bars offer front row seats for the street theater …

From the upper floors of the Rivoli you can enjoy an unrestricted view of the Rambla.

21

In the area

The Gran Via de les Corts Catalanes marks the boundary between the historic city center and the neighborhood of the Eixample, the 'extension' built at the end of the 19th century along the lines of a checkerboard. This district, one of the most thriving shopping areas in

Where to stay

Hotel Ritz (13)
Gran Via de les Corts Catalanes, 668 - 08010
☎ 93 318 52 00 ➡ 93 318 01 48

Ⓜ *Passeig de Gràcia, Urquinaona* 🔲 *148 rooms (13 suites)* ●●●●● ▢ ▣ ▦
▦ ⊞ ⊠ ⊕ ⊗ ▨ @ *www.ritzbcn.com*

As tradition demands, the Ritz, opened in 1919, is the most elegant of Barcelona's classic hotels: a vast entrance hall leading to a monumental double curved staircase, spacious rooms with Regency style furnishings, impeccable service and every comfort.

Gran Hotel Havana (14)
Gran Via de les Corts Catalanes, 647 - 08010
☎ 93 412 11 15 ➡ 93 412 26 11

Ⓜ *Passeig de Gràcia, Urquinaona* 🅿 *141 rooms (4 suites)* ●●●● ▣ ▢ ▦ ▦
▦ ⊞ ⊠ ⊕ @ *www.hoteles-silken.com*

Housed in a building dating from 1872, the Havana was converted into a hotel for the Olympic Games. The decoration reflects the most avant-garde trends in Catalan design, as evidenced by the amazing stained-glass window which lights up the entrance hall. All the rooms have been soundproofed and the bathrooms, decorated in steel and marble, are especially sophisticated. The hotel gives over an entire floor to business travelers, who will find all the equipment they need in each suite.

Hotel Duques de Bergara (15)
Carrer Bergara 11 - 08002 ☎ 93 301 51 51 ➡ 93 317 34 42

Ⓜ *Catalunya 140 rooms (3 suites)* ●●●● ▢ ▣ ▢ ▦ ▦ ▦ ▦ ⊞ ⊠ ⊕ ▨
▧ @ *www.hoteles-catalonia.es*

This Modernist building, designed at the end of the 19th century by the architect Emilio Salas, has been totally refurbished and equipped with all the most up-to-date facilities. Located right next to the Plaça de Catalunya, it is part of the Eixample's famous 'Quadrat d'Or' (golden square). The tone is set from the start: the paneled ceiling and Art-Deco stained glass of the entrance hall, the marble of the staircase, the carved wooden doors to the rooms, the functional designer furniture … The swimming pool is very inviting in summer.

Hotel Catalunya Plaça (16)
Plaça de Catalunya, 7 - 08002 ☎ 93 317 71 71 ➡ 93 317 78 55

Ⓜ *Catalunya 46 rooms* ●●● ▢ ▣ ▢ ▦ ⊞ ⊠ ⊕ ▨ @ *www.city-hotels.es*

This recently modernized hotel occupies a privileged position in the nerve center of the city. Its comfort and reasonable prices are worthy of note. Choose the rooms overlooking the square to take advantage of the view. No restaurant.

Not forgetting

■ **Hotel NH Calderón (17)** Rambla de Catalunya 26 - 08007
☎ 93 301 00 00 ➡ 93 412 41 93 ●●● *Central, practical and recently renovated hotel. Designer decoration and excellent service.*

the whole city, is an ideal base for exploring Barcelona.

The rooms at the Ritz are among the most luxurious Barcelona has to offer.

The monotony of the Eixample neighborhood, based on a plan drawn up by the engineer Ildefons Cerdà i Sunyer in the 1850s, is broken by the cluster of Modernist masterworks in the 'Quadrat d'Or' (golden square), bounded by the Carrer Aribau, the Passeig de Sant Joan, the

Where to stay

Hotel Claris (18)
Carrer Pau Claris 150 - 08009 ☎ 93 487 62 62 ➠ 93 215 79 70

Ⓜ *Passeig de Gràcia* Ⓟ *106 rooms (18 suites)* ●●●●● ▢ ▣ 🖾 🔝 Ⅲ 🏛
🍸 ✚ 🚭 🎿 *sauna, solarium* 🏊 @ www.derbyhotels.es

The conversion of the old palace of the Counts of Vedruna into a luxury hotel combines tradition and modernity: the neoclassical façade, put up in the 19th century at the height of Barcelona's 'Renaissance', is set off by a metal facing; the entrance hall mixes unadorned concrete, marble, exotic woods, modern furniture and 4th-century Roman mosaics; finally, the soundproofed rooms, designed and furnished by prestigious contemporary architects and interior decorators, also flaunt a resolutely modern style, in sharp contrast to the beautiful antique furniture. It is thus an ideal haunt for art lovers, especially as the hotel also has an exquisite collection of pieces from Ancient Egypt.

Gallery Hotel (19)
Carrer Rosselló 249 - 08008 ☎ 93 415 99 11 ➠ 93 415 91 84

Ⓜ *Diagonal* Ⓟ *108 rooms (5 suites)* ●●●● ▢ ▣ 🖾 Ⅲ 🏛 🍸 🖵 ✚ 🎿 ⚲
✚ *for banquets and conferences* 🚭 🎿 *sauna* 🏊 @ www.galleryhotel.com

Its location, near Barcelona's most famous monuments and smartest shopping area, is undoubtedly its main attraction. However, the Gallery also caters for traveling business people, as it is right next to the Avinguda Diagonal, the main artery of the commercial district and the site of many company offices. Comfort is guaranteed in all the rooms, which have functional furniture and are of a good size. When the weather is fine, breakfast can be taken on the superb terrace.

Hotel Condes de Barcelona (20)
Passeig de Gràcia 75 - 08008 ☎ 93 488 11 52 ➠ 93 487 14 42

Ⓜ *Passeig de Gràcia, Diagonal* Ⓟ *180 rooms (2 suites)* ●●●● ▢ ▣ 🖾 Ⅲ
🏛 ⚲ ✚ ✚ 🚭 🎿 *solarium* 🏊 @ www.condesdebarcelona.com

Ensconced in a Modernist building overlooking the Passeig de Gràcia, a few feet from the Pedrera and the Casa Batlló ➠ 95, the Condes has been beautifully modernized and soundproofed. On first crossing the threshold, it is impossible not to be won over by the amazing pentagonal entrance hall, lined with marble and lit by an enormous chandelier, a perfect introduction to the sophisticated rooms. Give in to the temptation of the swimming pool, if only to enjoy the view of the beautiful buildings along the avenue. It has an enviable reputation, and so it is a good idea to book well ahead.

■ **Hotel Majestic (21)** Passeig de Gràcia, 70 - 08008 ☎ 93 488 17 17 ➠ 93 488 18 80 ●●●● *A stylish, recently renovated neoclassical building, which boasts an excellent location in the heart of Barcelona's shopping district. It is difficult to resist the temptation to shop here, especially as some of the most prestigious fashion stores are installed on the ground floor.*
■ **Hotel Diplomatic (22)** Carrer Pau Claris, 122 - 08009 ☎ 93 488 02 00 ➠ 93 488 12 22 ●●●● *Centrally located hotel, equipped to provide the utmost comfort and, considering its category, very reasonably priced.*

Rondes and the Diagonal.

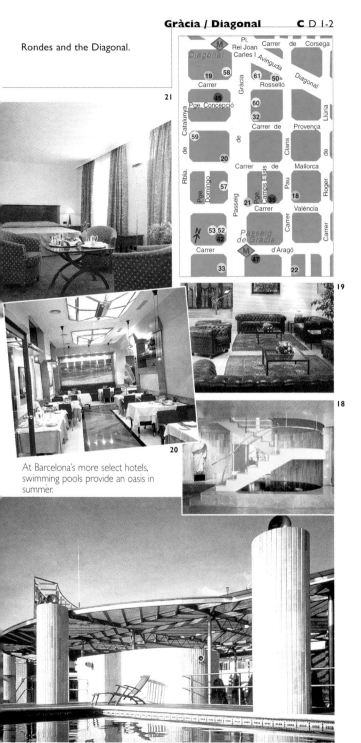

21

Pl.
Rei Joan Carles I
Carrer de Corsega
Diagonal
Avinguda
19 58
61 50
Carrer
Gràcia
Rosselló
Diagonal
45
Pge. Concepció
60
Llúria
32
Catalunya
Carrer de Provença
59
de
Claris
de
de
20
Rbla.
Carrer de Mallorca
Domingo
Pau
Roger
Pge.
57
Camps Elisis
18
Passeig
21 35
Carrer València
53 52
Carrer
Carrer
N
42
Passeig de Gràcia
Carrer d'Aragó
Carrer
33
47
22

19

18

At Barcelona's more select hotels, swimming pools provide an oasis in summer.

20

18

The city's three highest hotels, which yield the most beautiful panoramas in town from their top floors, are also among the most luxurious. Their special attraction derives not only from their irreproachable service and comfort but also the huge range of facilities they have on offer.

➡ Where to stay

Hotel Arts (23)
Carrer Marina, 19/21 - 08005 ☎ 93 221 10 00 → 93 221 10 70

Ⓜ *Marina* Ⓟ **397 rooms** *(58 suites)* ●●●●● ▢ ▣ ▨ ▨ ▥ ▦ *'Newport room'* ▢ ✖ ♿ *in some rooms and communal salons* ✚ ▨ ≋ *open air and heated* ▨ @ *www.harts.es*

A five-star establishment worthy of the famous Ritz-Carlton Hotels and Resorts international chain to which it belongs. With its thirty-three floors (500 feet), this iron and glass structure is, along with its neighbor, the Mapfre Tower, the highest skyscraper in the whole of Spain. The rooms obviously boast the most up-to-date equipment and the three top floors (CLUB category) have their own top-class room service! Choose the rooms overlooking the sea: the view of the bay and the Mediterranean is awe-inspiring. Business travelers can use a conference room with a capacity of 1,500 people.

Hotel Rey Juan Carlos Primero (24)
Avinguda Diagonal, 661 - 08028 ☎ 93 448 08 08 → 93 448 06 07

Ⓜ *Zona Universitaria* Ⓟ **375 rooms** *(37 suites)* ●●●●● ▢ ▣ ▨ ▥ ▦ ▦ *'Chez Vous' and 'Café Polo'* ▨ ✖ ♿ *communal rooms* ≋ *covered and open air* ▦ ▨ @ *www.hilton.com; hotel@hrjuancarlos.com*

The green areas, the Olympic swimming pool and the little artificial lake, complete with swans, are the most striking features of this elegant hotel, which occupies an enormous tower. The remarkable view of the whole city only adds to its charms: the efficient service and the facilities befit a luxury hotel … as do the shops in the vast entrance hall, which sell furs, jewelry and flowers, without forgetting the limousines … Gourmets will appreciate the Chez Vous restaurant, which champions French cuisine.

Hotel Princesa Sofia Intercontinental (25)
Plaça Pius XII, 4 - 08028 ☎ 93 330 71 11 ➡ 93 330 76 21

Ⓜ *Maria Cristina* Ⓟ *500 rooms* (21 suites) ●●●●● ▭ Ⓞ ▣ ☎ Ⓗ Ⅲ ⌗
'Snack buffet 2002' Ⓨ *'May Fair'* ⊞ ✂ sauna, beauty parlor ≋ *covered and open air* ⚘ Ⓐ www.interconti.com

The Princesa Sofia, HQ of the Olympic Committee during the 1992 Games, offers all the comforts of a top- rank hotel, and business people will find all the facilities they require. In fact, everything is done to make their life easier: twenty-one conference rooms are equipped with video projectors and simultaneous translation booths, and the large hall can seat 1,200 people. Its location, in the hub of Barcelona's financial and business activity, and close to its big shopping centers, is another advantage. Do not miss the Top City beauty parlor, on the nineteenth floor, which offers a view to take your breath away …

In the area

The Plaça Espanya is very strategically situated: it has immediate access not only to the motorways and airport but also to the city center, along the Gran Via de les Corts Catalanes. This sector's vitality is mainly due to the trade fairs and congresses which are held in the Recinte Firal, a

Where to stay

Barcelona Plaza Hotel (26)
Plaça Espanya, 6 - 08014 ☎ 93 420 26 00 ➡ 93 426 04 00

M *Espanya* P *338 rooms (9 suites)* ●●●● ▭ ▣ ☎ 🔌 Ⅲ 🍴 🍷 🖥 🚻 ✚
💾 ✖ *sauna and solarium* ≋ @ *www.hoteles-catalonia.es*

This modern hotel, which opened in 1993, faces on to the Plaça Espanya, directly opposite the Avinguda Reina Maria Cristina, the main artery of the Fira area: an ideal watering-hole for business people. The rooms are comfortable and functional: the suites are fitted out with an office. Do not forget to reserve a room ahead ...

Hotel Fira Palace (27)
Avinguda Rius i Taulet, 1 - 08004 ☎ 93 426 22 23 ➡ 93 424 86 79

M *Espanya* **258 rooms** *(18 suites)* ●●●● ▭ ▣ ☎ 🔌 Ⅲ 🍴 🍷 🚻 ✚ 💾
✖ ≋ *covered* @ *www.fira-palace.com*

The range of services on offer recommends this hotel to business travelers who are passing through Barcelona to attend the shows, seminars, congresses and suchlike which take place within the Recinte Firal and the Congress Hall. Some conferences are even organized in the halls of the Fira Palace itself, which have a capacity of 1,300 people. The emphasis of the rooms is on comfort and practicality. The sports room and the swimming pool provide a very welcome chance to relax between meetings!

Hotel Barceló Sants (28)
Plaça dels Països Catalans, s/n - 08014
☎ 93 490 95 95 ➡ 93 490 60 45

M *Sants Estació* P **364 rooms** *(13 suites)* ●●● ▭ ▣ ☎ 🔌 Ⅲ 🚻 ✚ 💾
@ *hotelbsants@wsite.es*

Its location, above Barcelona's main railroad station, is particularly suited to business guests, who are in an ideal spot for the airport and some after-hours relaxation in the city center, or an exploration of the surrounding neighborhood.

Expo Hotel (29)
Carrer Mallorca, 1 - 08014 ☎ 93 325 12 12 ➡ 93 325 11 44

M *Sants Estació* P **435 rooms** ●● ▭ ▣ ☎ Ⅲ 🍴 🖥 ✚ 💾 ≋
@ *comercialbcn@expogrupo.com*

A very large hotel near Sants station, a favorite for business people, who are attracted by its wide selection of facilities. Its spacious and comfortable conference rooms often play host to congresses. Choose the rooms overlooking the square, as they have more light.

Not forgetting

■ **Hotel Roma (30)** Avinguda de Roma, 31 - 08029 ☎ 93 410 66 33 ➡ 93 410 13 52 ●● *Hotel totally adapted to the needs of business guests: efficient service and functional rooms, although they are all furnished differently.*
■ **Hotel Abbot (31)** Avinguda de Roma, 23 - 08029 ☎ 93 430 04 05 ➡ 93 419 57 41 ●●● *A strategic position for this modern fully equipped hotel.*

leftover from the 1929 International Exhibition. As a result, the hotels especially aim to cater for the demands of business travelers.

30

27

28

26

27

The monumental façade of the Plaza Hotel dominates the Plaça Espanya in the heart of the trade fair district.

In the area

This very long avenue, linking the sea to Pedralbes, audaciously cleaves the grid of the Eixample, hence its name of 'diagonal'. Its upper zone, the most select, has been taken over by company offices: it is now Barcelona's foremost district for business and finance.

Where to stay

Hotel Hilton (32)
Avinguda Diagonal 589-591, 08014 ☎ 93 495 77 77 ➡ 93 495 77 00

Ⓜ *Maria Cristina* Ⓟ *286 rooms (2 suites)* ●●●● ▢ ◍ ▣ ☎ *with secretarial telephone service* ▥ ▤ ▥ ▦ *'Cristal'* Ⓨ *'Atrium'* ⓦ ✪ ♿ ✚ *for banquets and conferences* ✂ ⊞ @ *hilton@lix.intercom.es*

A very modern building, situated on the main road to the airport, very close to the Congress Hall and the trade fairs. This tastefully decorated hotel, is designed to satisfy the most exacting demands of its business guests: a modem has been installed in every room for Internet access, and 15 conference rooms are available for meetings and seminars. There is a beautiful view of the city from the upper floors.

Hotel Derby (33)
Carrer Loreto 21/25 - 08029 ☎ 93 322 32 15 ➡ 93 410 08 62

▣ *15* Ⓟ *107 rooms (4 suites)* ●●● ▢ ◍ ▣ ☎ ▥ *modem* ▤ ▥ *safe* ▦ Ⓨ *'Scotch Bar'* ✚ *for banquets and conferences* @ *www.derbyhotels.es*

Tucked away in a very quiet street, ideal for anybody who wants to escape the tumult of the nearby Diagonal, the Hotel Derby appeals to both tourists and business people. Recently refurbished, it boasts state of the art rooms set on two levels.

Hotel Melià (34)
Avinguda Sarrià 50 - 08029 ☎ 93 410 60 60 ➡ 93 321 51 79

▣ *66* Ⓟ *308 rooms (4 suites)* ●●●● ▢ ▣ ☎ ▤ ▥ ▦ ⓦ ✚ *for banquets and conferences* ▨ @ *www.solmeliá.es*

Its location, near the offices and the trade fairs, a mere stroll away from good restaurants and big shopping centers (El Corte Inglés, the Illa Diagonal), is one of the main attractions of this very large hotel. The facilities, and the possibility of organizing meetings and seminars, have made it popular with business people. There is a wonderful view of Barcelona from the rooms on the upper floors.

Hotel L'Illa (35)
Avinguda Diagonal, 555 - 08029 ☎ 93 410 33 00 ➡ 93 410 88 92

Ⓜ *Maria Cristina 103 rooms* (10 suites) ●●●● ▢ ▣ ☎ ▥ ⓦ ♿ ✚ ▨ ⊞

This recently built hotel is part of the Illa shopping complex, which has won several architectural prizes. The rooms are comfortable – especially recommended are the rooms on the top floors overlooking the avenue, with their view of the skyscrapers dotted along the Diagonal.

N.H. Forum (36)
Carrer Ecuador, 20 - 08029 ☎ 93 419 36 36 ➡ 93 419 89 10

▣ *43, 78 47 rooms (1 suite)* ●● ▢ ▣ ☎ ▥ ▦ ⓦ ✚ ▨

A part of one of the most important chains in Spain, synonymous with comfortable modern hotels, the Forum has a policy of moderate pricing – not something to be dismissed lightly!

Although situated right at the heart of the trade fair district, the Hilton is an oasis of peace with the guarantee of a well-earned rest between meetings ... or visits to the city's tourist attractions.

A trap for vegetarians

Amanida mixta: mixed salad, very enticing for anybody who wants to avoid eating meat. However, in among the tomatoes and lettuce leaves, you may be surprised by anchovies or pieces of diced ham. If you want a strictly vegetarian dish, order an amanida verda.

➡ Where to eat

Glossary of Catalan gastronomic terms

all i oli: strong garlic mayonnaise
calçotada: grilled green onions with *salsa romesco* (see below)
calderet: fish and shellfish stew
carn d'olla: mixed meat soup
escudella: mixed meat and vegetable soup
fideuà: noodles cooked in fish broth
salsa romesco: spicy tomato and almond sauce
suquets: fish casserole
trinxat: dish of chopped vegetables

Catalan cuisine

Catalan cuisine has earned a rightful place among the most respected in Europe: the sea provides its fish and its prosperous hinterland supplies the other fresh ingredients. Outstanding among the latter are the wild mushrooms: when they are in season, no meal can be considered complete without them!

72 Restaurants

THE INSIDER'S FAVORITES

The number of taverns serving tapas (pastries or hors d'œuvre eaten before a main meal) is constantly on the increase in Barcelona. Basque bars, renowned for their pintxos (snacks picked up with a toothpick) are the most popular at the moment. The formula is simple: just take your choice from the dishes lined up on the bar and pay at the end, stating

Where to eat

Irati (1)
Carrer Cardenal Casanyes, 17 - 08002 ☎ 93 302 30 84

Ⓜ *Liceu* ● ▤ Ⓞ *Tue.–Sat. noon–4pm, 7pm–midnight; Sun. noon–4pm*

Typical Basque tavern; every day, before lunch and in the evening around 8pm, the bar is covered with an array of plates and bowls filled with *chistorras* (small sausages), *pimientos de piquillo* (stuffed peppers), fried fish, pastries and several kinds of salads and sauces, accompanied by Rioja (red wine), Txacoli (Basque white wine) or *zurritos*. Irati also has a dining-room which serves Basque specialties (especially fish dishes), prepared with high-quality ingredients. Set menus from Mondays to Fridays: 2,200 Ptas.

Euskal Etxea (2)
Placeta Montcada, 1/3 - 08003 ☎ 93 310 21 85

Ⓜ *Jaume I* ● ▤ Ⓞ *Tue.–Sat. noon–4pm, 6pm–midnight; Sun. noon–4pm*

A very beautiful Basque tavern, situated in a typical back street, which was one of the first to launch the fashion for pintxos in Barcelona. These days it is always full just before lunchtime – especially on weekends. A host of specialties: fried fish, sausages and black puddings, salads and peppers; excellent house wines. There is also a dining-room, with a menu of Basque specialties. The Euskal Etxea often puts on exhibitions and book presentations.

the number of tapas you have tried! And wash them all down with a glass of wine or a *zurrito* (small beer).

4

Xampanyet (3)
Carrer Montcada, 22 - 08003
☎ 93 319 70 03

🅼 *Jaume I* ● 🖪 🕓 *Tue.–Sun. noon–4pm, 6.30pm–midnight*

One of the city's oldest and best known tapas bars, decorated with colorful traditional tiles. It takes its name from a cocktail based on cava ➡ 112 (Catalan champagne), the recipe for which is handed down from father to son and jealously guarded ... You will certainly have to eat standing up, as there are only a few tables (the bar is tiny), but it is well worth any discomfort. Good fish dishes.

Tapa Tapa (4)
Passeig de Gràcia, 44 - 08007 ☎ 93 488 33 69

🅼 *Passeig de Gràcia* ● 🖪 🕓 *daily 8am–1am* 🔳

Opened in 1993, the Tapa Tapa started the trend for big tapas bars on the Passeig de Gràcia. The enormous space offers a vast range of salads, croquettes, charcuterie (cold meats), cheeses, squids, snails and all kinds of pastries, swilled down with German or Irish beers. On fine days, the tables are placed outside, on the elegant Passeig de Gràcia, where they make an even prettier sight.

Not forgetting
🔳 **Txapela (Euskal taberna) (5)** Passeig de Gràcia, 8/10 - 08007 ☎ 93 412 02 89 ● 🕓 *daily 8am–11.30pm A new bar, furnished in typical Basque style, which offers a great variety of pintxos and a huge selection of wines, especially Riojas.*

In the area

The oldest part of the city is packed with small traditional restaurants which show off the fresh local produce on sale in Barcelona's best market, the Boqueria. For visitors in a rush, the neighborhood also contains a large number of less typical eateries which serve a wide

Where to eat

Cal Pep (6)
Plaça de les Olles, 8 - 08003 ☎ 93 310 79 61

Ⓜ Jaume I **Catalan cuisine** ● ▣ 🕐 *Tue.–Sat. 8am–midnight; Mon. 6pm–midnight; closed public holidays*

You can choose between a bar groaning with wonderful tapas, for a light and informal meal, in a small friendly room, or a taste of seafood specialties and dishes from the Catalan heartland, for a reasonable price. Not to be missed: fried tuna with potatoes, squids from the Costa Brava and meatballs with dried fruit, specialties of a popular cuisine in which the quality of the ingredients is its most attractive feature.

Café de la Academia (7)
Carrer Lledó 1 / Plaça de Sant Just - 08002 ☎ 93 319 82 53

Ⓜ Jaume I **Creative cuisine** 🗂 ●● ▣ 🕐 *Mon.–Fri. 1–4pm, 8.30pm–midnight; Sat. 8.30pm–midnight; closed public holidays* ✴

A fascinating restaurant which occupies an 18th-century building that lords it over the square and church of Sant Just. The elegant décor and the subdued atmosphere set off the ancient building's thick walls and the beautiful works of art hanging on them. The Academia offers an unusual and varied menu, using top quality products, and combining the influence of Mediterranean traditions with creative innovations. Try the rice cooked in sepia ink, the skewered bonito (a type of tuna) in bacon fat and chicory, or the quail stuffed with liver and onions. In summer dinner is served outside, in the square. It is advisable to book ahead.

Pitarra (8)
Carrer Avinyó, 56 - 08002 ☎ 93 301 16 47

Ⓜ Jaume I **Classic cuisine** ●● ▣ 🕐 *Mon.–Sat. 1–4pm, 8.30–11pm; public holidays 1–4pm*

A restaurant over one hundred years old, previously the site of the clock-making business of the poet Frederic Soler, the father of Catalan theater. It still houses an exquisite collection of watches, clocks and manuscripts, which the present owners Jaume and Marc Roig (the former overseeing the tables, the latter the kitchen) proudly display to their more inquisitive customers. A spot replete with history, it offers an abundant choice, with reasonably priced dishes and cheap set menus at lunchtime. Try the duck with mushrooms, the fish and seafood soup and, in season, game. For gluttons, a wonderful selection of desserts …

Not forgetting

◼ **Senyor Parellada (9)** Carrer Argentería, 37 - 08003 ☎ 93 319 30 33 Catalan cuisine ●● 🕐 *Mon.–Sat. 1–3.30pm, 8.30–11pm Restaurant located in a beautiful building in the neighborhood of La Ribera. Excellent rice dishes. Book ahead.* ◼ **El Gran Café (10)** Carrer Avinyó, 9 - 08002 ☎ 93 318 79 86 Catalan cuisine ●● 🕐 *Tue.–Sat. 1–4pm, 8.30–11pm; Sun. 1–4pm Art Deco rooms for a traditional menu influenced by French cooking. Worth a detour.* ◼ **Mastroqué (11)** Carrer Còdols, 29 - 08002 ☎ 93 301 79 42 Creative cuisine ●● 🕐 *Mon.–Sat. 1–4pm, 8.30–11pm New restaurant, in a back alley near the port. The choice of ingredients shows a certain French influence. The liver pâtés and the carpaccios are particularly good. Interesting wine list.*

variety of sandwiches at very
reasonable prices.

Like many
central
restaurants,
El Gran Cáfe
is richly
furnished in
period style.

In the area

Contrary to the impression given by its name, the Port Vell, or 'Old Port', is an area with long beaches and modern shopping centers which has given birth to a number of restaurants exploring Mediterranean cuisine. Since the 1980s it has become a favorite with local people.

Where to eat

Set Portes (12)
Passeig Isabel II, 14 - 08003 ☎ 93 319 30 33

Ⓜ *Barceloneta* **Classic cuisine** ●●● ▣ ▣ ◐ *daily 1pm–1am*

Founded in 1836, this prestigious restaurant is one of the most popular in the city. Located under the arches designed by Xifré, in a building of great architectural interest, it was one of the first to have running water and was the subject of the first photograph ever taken in Spain. It comprises several dining-rooms, some of them private; the largest, and oldest, creates nostalgia for the restaurant's most eminent former customers, as their names are inscribed on the narrow seats. The menu, based on Catalan specialties, is particularly varied; do not miss the rice dishes, which the chef reinvents every day, with the 'Perellada' fish risotto an absolute must. The hot and cold hors-d'œuvre and the seafood are also mouthwatering. Efficient service and an excellent wine céllar.

El Merendero de la Mari (13)
Plaça Pau Vila, 1 - 08039 ☎ 93 221 31 41

Ⓜ *Barceloneta* **Fish specialties** ●● ▣ ◐ *Mon.–Sat. 1–4pm, 8.30–11pm; Sun. 1–4pm* ▣

Housed in the ground floor of the Palau de Mar, the site of the Museu d'Història de Catalunya, facing out on the Port Vell, El Merendero stands out from the other fish restaurants in the neighborhood on account of its elegant and highly colorful décor, its service and the quality of its cuisine. When it is particularly hot, the sea breeze makes meals on the terrace very pleasant … and the view of the wharves only adds to the charm! The menu features traditional coastal recipes. The fried fish, *suquets* (fish casseroles) and rice dishes are outstanding, but the cod *buñuelos* (fritters), black rice cooked in sepia ink and burbot in *fideuà* (noodles cooked in fish stock) are equally worthy of note. When the weather is good, booking ahead is highly advisable!

Real Club Maritim (14)
Moll d'Espanya, s/n - 08039 ☎ 93 221 71 43

▣ *19,40* **Classic cuisine** ●●● ▣ ▣ ◐ *Mon.–Sat. 1–4pm, 8.30–11pm*

The proximity of Maremagnum, the enormous shopping complex which contains a host of bars, restaurants and fast-food joints, does not seem to have affected the Real Club: it has lost none of the allure and elegance of its early days. There is no need to have a sailboat anchored in the harbor to enjoy a romantic meal overlooking the sea! This sophisticated setting, reminiscent of an officers' club, is matched by the attentive service and continental cooking, based on fresh fish, seafood and rice. Try the eggplants with goat's cheese and the sea bream in apple and cider sauce.

Not forgetting

■ **Can Majó (15)** Carrer Almirall Aixada, 23 - 08003 ☎ 93 221 54 55 Fish specialties ●● ◐ *Tue.–Sun. 1–4pm, 8.30–11pm Famous restaurant which serves good fish and seafood, including an excellent suquet.* ■ **Paco Alcalde (16)** Carrer Almirall Aixada, 12 - 08003 ☎ 93 221 50 26 Fish specialties ●●● ◐ *Wed.–Mon. 1–4pm, 8.30–11pm Particulary appetizing suquets, caderetes (fish stews) and fideuas.*

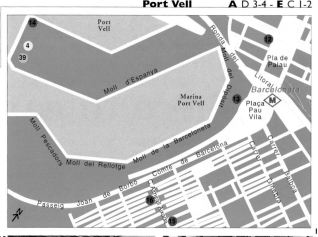

In the area

This neighborhood, which was completely refurbished for the 1992 Olympic Games, is now Barcelona's architectural showcase: a new sports complex, avant-garde skyscrapers, sculpture by Frank Gehry ... And the countless restaurants and designer bars, very inviting after the beach in

Where to eat

Talaia Mar (17)
Carrer Marina, 16 - 08005 ☎ 93 221 90 90

Ⓜ Ciutadella **Creative cuisine** ▮ ●●●● ▯ Ⓢ *daily 1–4pm, 8.30–11pm* ▨

This restaurant, with its strange circular layout and designer furniture, in the shadow of the Mapfre tower, provides an excellent spread: the ingredients are of a high quality, the wine list is more than satisfactory, the desserts are surprising and the service is courteous. The 'fast formula', which makes it possible to eat in 45 minutes, caters to the requirements of business meals without ever sacrificing quality. What is more, the sense of sight is as stimulated as the sense of taste, thanks to the wonderful view of the sea.

Agua (18)
Passeig Marítim de la Barceloneta, 30 - 08005 ☎ 93 225 12 72

Ⓜ Ciutadella **Creative cuisine** ●● ▯ Ⓢ *daily 1–4pm, 8.30–11pm* ▣

One of Barcelona's most fashionable restaurants. Once its customers have entered the door opening onto the boulevard, they go down a corridor and suddenly find themselves almost paddling in water ... in a sunny room with a breathtaking view of the sea. In good weather they can even eat on the beach, by the light of candles and lanterns. The décor represents a harmonious mixture of colonial and rural styles. The cuisine, inspired by Mediterranean ingredients, is simple but tasty: you will not be disappointed by the carpaccios, salads or fish dishes. It is advisable to book ahead.

El Tunel del Port (19)
Moll de Gregal, 12 - 08005 ☎ 93 221 03 21

Ⓜ Ciutadella **Fish specialties** ●●● ▮ ▯ Ⓢ *Tue.–Sat. 1–4pm, 8.30–11.30pm; Sun. 1–4pm* ▣

El Tunel stands out from the many fish restaurants in the Olympic port through the quality of its ingredients, the friendliness of the service and a sophisticated modern atmosphere. Its large bay windows look out on the sea, and it is also possible to eat under the stars ... The paellas, *fideuas* and rice in sepia ink are all outstanding. To fully appreciate this spot, come during the week, as it's less hectic than on weekends ...

Restaurante del Teatre Nacional (20)
Plaça de les Arts, 1 - 08013 ☎ 93 306 57 00

Ⓜ Glòries **Classic cuisine** ●● ▮ ▯ Ⓢ *Tue.–Sun. 8pm–2am*

Recently installed in Barcelona's brand new theater ➡ 68, this tastefully decorated restaurant has the advantage of staying open late, to catch the audiences coming out of the shows. Set menus or à la carte.

Not forgetting

■ **Xiringuito Escribà (21)** Litoral Mar, 42 - 08013 ☎ 93 221 07 29 Fish specialties ●● Ⓢ *Tue.–Thu. 11am–6pm; Fri.–Sun. 11am–11.30pm Owned by the Escribà family, traditional cake and chocolate makers, the Xiringuito has both a restaurant and a cafeteria. An impressive choice of tapas, fish dishes and paellas.*

summer, have long since replaced the *chiringuitos* (greasy spoons).

19

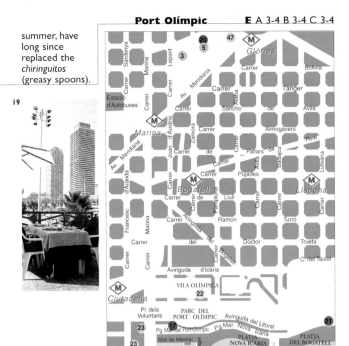

21

In the area

The Rambla is undoubtedly Barcelona's most distinctive thoroughfare, the artery through which its lifeblood races. The restaurants which grace this famous stage all, in their own way, have a story to tell about the capital of Catalonia.

Where to eat

Amaya (22)
Rambla, 24 - 08002 ☎ 93 302 10 37

Ⓜ *Liceu* **Regional cuisine** 🔲 ●● ▭ 🕐 **tapas** daily 11am–4.30pm, 7pm–midnight **restaurant** daily 1pm–5pm, 8.30pm–midnight **cafeteria** daily 9am–midnight

A famous eating house, with a somewhat austere classical feel, in which the knowledgeable and highly regarded chef combines elements of the Basque and Catalan traditions: pintxos, delicatessen, salads and other more complicated dishes at the bar, seafood (salt cod and clams) and paellas to be enjoyed in the restaurant. Very good wine cellar.

Los Caracoles (23)
Carrer Escudellers, 14 - 08002 ☎ 93 302 31 85

Ⓜ *Liceu* **Classic cuisine** ●● ▭ 🕐 daily 1–4.30pm, 8.30–11.30pm

The rustic décor, the walls lined with mementos, the animated conversations, the home cooking which generally concentrates on meat dishes (lamb and grilled chicken) – this is definitely a typical Barcelona haunt, which has managed to retain all the charm and atmosphere of an old-world tavern. However, success has its price, so be patient and weave your way through the throng for an aperitif at the bar before sitting down for your meal …

Les Quinze Nits (24)
Plaça Reial, 6 - 08002 ☎ 93 317 30 75

Ⓜ *Liceu* **Catalan cuisine** ● ▭ 🕐 daily 1–4pm, 8.30–11.30pm

Simple modern décor in this pleasant restaurant, nestling under the arches of the beautiful Plaça Reial (ask for a table on the upper floor to take full advantage of the view). It has one of the best quality/price ratios in Barcelona – and it shows: as the Quinze Nits does not accept bookings, the line often trickles several feet out of the door. However, it is always worth the wait: a huge selection of Catalan specialties – tuna cannelloni, *fideuà* – and delicious desserts.

Egipte (25)
La Rambla, 79 - 08002 ☎ 93 317 74 80

Ⓜ *Liceu* **Fish specialties** ● ▭ 🕐 Mon.–Sat. 1–4pm, 8.30–11.30pm; Sun. 1–4pm

A very lively restaurant, with dishes which do full justice to the fresh produce from the nearby Boqueria market ➡ 138. A wide range of dishes based on salt cod. Set menus at lunchtime. Book ahead.

Not forgetting

■ **El Turia (26)** Carrer Petxina, 7 - 08001 ☎ 93 317 95 09 Classic cuisine ●● 🕐 Tue.–Sat. 1–4.30pm, 8.30–11.30pm; Sun. 1–4.30pm *A popular restaurant which offers produce from the Boqueria at reasonable prices.*
■ **Can Culleretes (27)** Carrer Quintana, 5 - 08002 ☎ 93 317 64 85 Catalan cuisine ● 🕐 Tue.–Sat. 1–4.30pm, 8.30–11.30pm; Sun. 1–4.30pm *Souvenirs and photographs chronicle a hundred years of history here. The helpings are generous … and the bill modest!*

Catalunya M

Rbla. Canaletes

2

37
34 31

C. Elisabets

6
8 36 Pl. Vila
de Madrid

35

Rbla. Estudis

7
Fortuny

9

Carrer Pintor

15

C. Portaferrissa

32

Carrer del Carme

17

31

Rbla. Sant Josep

Mercat de
la Boqueria

43

29

13

Carrer Patxina

30

Carrer de l'Hospital

Pl. Sant
Agustí

Pla de la
Boqueria

28

C. Boqueria

29

Rbla. dels Caputxins

Liceu M

C. Colom

12 Sant Pau

10

1

14 27

Carrer Ferran

24 6

Carrer de Sant Pau

11

10 25

Rbla.

45

26

Carrer Nou de la Rambla

34

27
Teatre

Pl. C. Escudellers

23

9

Carrer Art del Teatre

Rbla. Santa Mònica

Avinguda de Les Drassanes

22

23

Rbla.

28

21

Drassanes

Plaça
Portal de
la Pau

Avinguda del Paral·lel

27

24

22

27

23

25

25

In the area

The popular Raval neighborhood, in the heart of the old city, is less famous than others, but it is worth exploring as it also boasts back streets full of charm and some excellent restaurants.

Where to eat

Casa Leopoldo (28)
Carrer Sant Rafael, 24 - 08001 ☎ 93 441 30 14

M *Sant Antoni* **Catalan cuisine** ●●● ⬛ *Tue.–Sat. 1–4.30pm, 8.30–11.30pm; Sun. 1–4.30pm*

This restaurant, which has been run by the same family since 1929, has lost count of the celebrities who have crossed its threshold ... The rustic décor of *azulejos* (wall tiles) depicting scenes from country life, bullfights and old Barcelona reflect regional cooking which takes pride in the quality of its ingredients, all meticulously prepared. The extremely varied menu proposes combinations which are often surprising. The service is attentive and the wine cellar has a high reputation. It is advisable to book ahead.

Can Lluis (29)
Carrer Cera, 49 - 08001 ☎ 93 441 11 87

M *Sant Antoni* **Catalan cuisine** ● ⬛ *Mon.–Sat. 1–4.30pm, 8.30–11.30pm; cafeteria: Mon.–Sat. 1–11.30pm*

A family restaurant which creates popular home cooking with top-quality ingredients, adapted to seasonal availability. At lunchtime it offers a set menu with a good quality/price ratio. The service is quick and efficient, ideal for a working lunch, or for not losing too much time in a busy sightseeing schedule! If the owner, unmoved by any fleeting trends, has opted for simple, unadorned decoration, it is because he wants his customers to pay full attention to what's on their plates ...

Casa Isidre (30)
Carrer Flors, 12 - 08001 ☎ 93 441 11 39

M *Paral.lel* **Catalan cuisine** ●● ⬛ *Mon.–Sat. 1–4.30pm, 8.30–11.30pm*

This is one of the restaurants most typical of the Raval neighborhood, with beautiful antique furnishings. The Isidre is very inconspicuous from the street, but the cognoscenti do not pass it by, for it serves top-quality food, with a huge selection of Catalan specialties, with emphasis on the fresh ingredients. Ignore the set menu and do not be overwhelmed by the wide choice, as the staff will help you make up your mind.

Pa i Trago (31)
Carrer Parlament, 41 - 08015 ☎ 93 441 13 20

M *Sant Antoni* **Catalan cuisine** ●● ⬛ *Tue.–Sun. 1–4.30pm, 8.30–11.30pm*

In this traditional restaurant, with big wooden tables and posters from the turn of the century on the walls, the welcome is warm and the décor simple. The Pa i Trago, which is in a class of its own for sausages and meat, offers excellent cooking while respecting Catalan traditions. Try the particularly tasty tripe with pig's feet! The lunchtime set menu (2,500 Ptas) is varied and one of the most complete, making it possible for the enthusiastic diner to become acquainted with some of the jewels in the local gastronomic crown.

Paellas and *fideuas* are not exclusive to eastern Spain, and Barcelona's countless fish restaurants bear this out, for they are often inspired by recipes from Galicia and the Basque country, regions where, as in Catalonia, seafood is the main staple of the diet. Special treats include tasty *suquets*, excellent black rice, cooked in sepia ink, pike, and sea bream in a

Where to eat

Botafumeiro (32)
Carrer Gran de Gràcia, 81 - 08012 ☎ 93 218 42 30

Ⓜ *Fontana* ●●●● ▭ ◷ *daily 1.30–4.30pm, 8.30–11.30pm*

Botafumeiro, one of the city's most prestigious *marisquerias* (seafood restaurants), has one of the most wide-ranging selections of fish and seafood, freshly caught and cooked to order. The menu features many specialties from Galicia, including octopus, prepared in a variety of ways. The setting is sophisticated and the portions generous. The wine cellar, stocked from Catalan and Galician vineyards, is enhanced by good whites, such as Ribiero and Turbio. The desserts are no less inviting! Do not forget to make a reservation.

La Muscleria (33)
Carrer Mallorca, 290 - 08037 ☎ 93 458 98 44

Ⓜ *Verdaguer* ● ▭ ◷ *Tue.–Sat. 1–4pm, 8–11.30pm; Sun. 1–4pm*

As the name suggests, the menu here abounds in mussels, prepared from over twenty different recipes. Connoisseurs prefer them with bacon (Dutch style) or with Roquefort (the basis of 'tigri'). The fried mussel formula is always thought to be peculiar to more northern climes, but the Muscleria has proved that it can be adapted to Mediterranean tastes and has won over Catalan gourmets: the place is always packed, and the atmosphere exuberant. However, the

salt crust. Shrimp, prawns, lobsters and mollusks also adorn Barcelona's tables.

34

36

33

management has not forgotten those customers who may be allergic to mussels; they can choose from delicious fish dishes, with those based on salt cod being specially succulent. As for drinks, try the sangría – it's particularly good.

Carballeira (34)
Avinguda Reina Maria Cristina, 3 - 08003 ☎ 93 310 10 06

Ⓜ *Drassanes* ●●●● ▢ Ⓞ *Tue.–Sat. 1–4.30pm, 8–11.30pm*

Long-established brasserie which serves delicious examples of Galician cuisine. Their shellfish are generally of outstanding quality (the oysters are exceptional), as are the fish dishes: sole, sea bream and bass … Everything is cooked with the utmost simplicity and refinement and served in generous portions in elegant surroundings. The wine cellar is particularly well stocked with good vintages. Notwithstanding the ample size of the restaurant, you are urged to book ahead.

Not forgetting

■■ **Les Ostres (35)** Carrer Valencia, 267 - 08007 ☎ 93 215 30 35 ●●●
Ⓞ *Mon.–Sat. 1.30–4.30pm, 8.30–11.30pm The name gives it away: this restaurant mainly serves oysters, which are extremely fresh. Friendly atmosphere.*
■■ **Rias de Galicia (36)** Carrer Lleida, 7 - 08004 ☎ 93 424 81 52 ●●●
Ⓞ *daily 1.30–4.30pm, 8.30–11.30pm Fish and seafood specialties and traditional recipes from Galicia, such as octopus and lacón con grelos (shoulder of pork with turnip tops).* ■■ **Peixerot (37)** Carrer Tarragona, 177 - 08014
☎ 93 424 69 69 ●●● Ⓞ *Tue.–Sat. 1.30–4.30pm, 8.30pm–11.30pm; Sun. 1.30–4.30pm A restaurant which has been rechristened, on account of its rice dishes and sea bream.*

In the area

The Plaça de Catalunya is the city's epicenter, as indicated by the star in its center, made up of pink and gray paving stones. It contains a number of bars and fast-food joints, which offer set menus at lunchtime, as well as more prestigious restaurants, imbued with history, which serve a wide

Where to eat

Brasserie Fló (38)
Carrer Jonqueres, 10 - 08002 ☎ 93 319 31 02

Ⓜ Urquinaona **Creative cuisine** ●● ▢ 🕓 *daily 1.30–4pm, 8.30–11.30pm*

This pleasant brasserie is housed in an enormous old textile factory, and traces of its former industrial function have been beautifully preserved. It is decorated in Art-Deco style. The menu combines Catalan dishes with French recipes. Especially recommended: meats in sauce and the oysters. There is a reasonably priced set menu at night.

Laie Libreria Café (39)
Carrer Pau Clarís, 85 - 08010 ☎ 93 302 73 10

Ⓜ Urquinaona **Classic cuisine** 🗇 ●● ▢ 🕓 *Tue.–Sat. 9am–1am*

At first only a bookshop, ten years ago the Laie added a beautiful dining-room and cafeteria on the floor above. At lunchtime the self-service buffet offers a selection of salads, patés, rice dishes and daily specialties and desserts of the house. At night, on the other hand, you can eat in the restaurant itself and take advantage of an excellent menu. The management's cultural background means that there are also regular exhibitions, lectures and book presentations.

Casa Calvet (40)
Carrer Casp, 48 - 08010 ☎ 93 412 40 12

Ⓜ Urquinaona **Catalan cuisine** 🗇 ●●● ▢ 🕓 *Mon.–Sat. 1.30–4.30pm, 8.30–11.30pm; closed public holidays*

Ensconced in a building put up by the Modernist architect Antoni Gaudí in 1899, this restaurant occupies the old administrative offices of the famous Calvet textile company. Nothing in the décor seems to have changed since then: the exposed beams, the old-style stucco walls and the furniture, also the work of Gaudí, have all been lovingly preserved. The menu is sophisticated: it gives pride of place to top-quality ingredients and seeks to create combinations which are surprising but always intelligent, and never stray too far from Catalan tradition. It is topped off with an inspired wine list: you can be sure to find a vintage perfectly suited to any dish, at a reasonable price … A friendly welcome and irreproachable service.

La Maison du Languedoc Roussillon (41)
Carrer Pau Clarís, 77 - 08010 ☎ 93 310 498

Ⓜ Urquinaona **French cuisine** ●●●● 🕓 *Tue.–Fri. 1.30–4.30pm, 8.30–11.30pm; Sat. 1.30–4.30pm; closed public holidays*

Certainly not cheap, but the quality of the food fully justifies the prices. It comes as a surprise to find this restaurant in Barcelona, as the menu mainly consists of specialties from southwest France, although it also finds room for Catalan recipes … However, even these are modified in accordance with the culinary precepts prevailing on the other side of the Pyrenees, which is also the source of its fresh ingredients. All in all, an interesting menu to delve into. Furthermore, the management is keen to spread word of the cultural aspects of Languedoc-Roussillon, by putting on photographic exhibitions.

variety of more sophisticated meals.

38

39

40

39

41

In the area

The Passeig de Gràcia, the majestic hub of the Eixample, once dotted with inns, now boasts several Modernist buildings used as offices and luxury shops. In the last few years it has proved a popular location for restaurants, bars and tapas bars. The food on offer ranges from simple

Where to eat

Boix de la Cerdanya (42)
Passeig de Gràcia, 51 - 08007 ☎ 93 487 38 20

Ⓜ *Passeig de Gràcia* **Regional cuisine** ●● ▤ 🕐 *daily 1—4pm, 8.30pm–midnight*

The famous chef J. M. Boix, who made his name in Martinet de la Cerdanya, a Pyrenean village near Andorra, is in charge here. The food has a mountain feel, through such dishes as cauliflower *trinxat* (chopped vegetables), baked potatoes and lamb. The atmosphere is sophisticated but the prices are not excessive. The only problem is that the wine list is rather short.

Cytrus (43)
Passeig de Gràcia, 44 - 08007 ☎ 93 487 23 45

Ⓜ *Passeig de Gràcia* **Classic cuisine** ●● ▤ 🕐 *daily 1—4.30pm, 8.30–11.30pm*

This restaurant has not seen an empty table since it opened. Its success is due to the remarkable view of the famous avenue and its upper-class residences (Cytrus is on the first floor), the attentive service, the friendly atmosphere and, of course, the cuisine, which comprises intelligently assembled Mediterranean dishes at modest prices. Try the green asparagus salad with oil of Jabugo ham, fillet steak in Cabernet-Sauvignon and, for dessert, the mint *damablanca* (an exquisite juxtaposition of dark and white chocolate). It is essential to book ahead.

Semproniana (44)
Carrer Rosselló, 148 08036 - ☎ 93 453 18 20

Ⓜ *Diagonal* **Creative cuisine** 🗇 ●● ▤ 🕐 *Mon.–Sat. 1.30–4.30pm, 8.30–11.30pm; closed public holidays*

A surprising restaurant, ensconced in an old printing-house and run by a family who are masters of the culinary art. Particular care has been taken with the décor: the furniture, floor and lighting all tie in with the remaining vestiges of the building's former life. The menu, a fresh interpretation of Catalan tradition, will not let you down: try the black sausage lasagna, the squids and olives in sauce and the desserts. Book ahead.

Tragaluz (45)
Passatge de la Concepció, 5 - 08008 ☎ 93 487 06 21

Ⓜ *Diagonal* **Creative cuisine** ●●● ▤ 🕐 *Cafeteria daily 1.30–4.30pm, 8.30–1am; Restaurant daily 1.30–4.30pm, 8.30–11.30pm*

A fashionable spot, in a quiet alley in the Eixample's checkerboard. The ground floor cafeteria, next to the bar, offers reasonably priced Japanese snacks, while the restaurant, one floor up, serves Mediterranean cuisine in a designer setting by the artist Javier Mariscal.

Not forgetting

■ **Yamadori (46)** Carrer Aribau, 68 - 08007 ☎ 93 453 92 64 Japanese cuisine ●●● 🕐 *Tue.–Sat. 1.30–4.30pm, 8.30–11.30pm; Sun. 1.30–4.30pm Traditional restaurant with extremely attentive service.* ■ **Ca La Sila (47)** Carrer Aragón, 282 - 08007 ☎ 93 215 70 26 Fish specialpties ●●● 🕐 *daily 1.30–4pm, 8.30–11.30pm Good cooking at modest price. The atmosphere is friendly and lively. Advance reservations not accepted.*

snacks to more elaborate fare.

In the area

Although this business neighborhood has fewer restaurants than some others, it still contains some very good places to eat: restaurants with a long history of preparing refined regional cuisine, or brasseries offering simpler fare – daily 'specials' and a variety of tasty sandwiches.

Where to eat

L'Olivé (48)
Carrer Muntaner, 171 - 08036 ☎ 93 430 90 27

Ⓜ *Hospital Clínic* **Classic cuisine** ●● ▣ 🕙 *Mon.–Sat. 1–4pm, 8.30pm–midnight; Sun. 1–4pm*

A traditional restaurant unmatched on the Catalan gastronomic scene. Among the most mouthwatering dishes, which come in generous portions, are the cannelloni, the *escudella* (meat and vegetable soup served with pasta) and *vedella amb bolets* (veal with mushrooms). The wine list is particularly extensive and the desserts, including an unforgettable *crema catalana* (crème caramel), are expertly prepared. The rooms are furnished in a classical and unostentatious style. The service is attentive and courteous. It is advisable to book ahead, especially on weekends, as the locals are assiduous regulars here…

El Barkito (49)
Carrer Córsega, 225 - 08036 ☎ 93 430 51 60

Ⓜ *Diagonal, Hospital Clínic* **Fish specialties** ●● ▣ 🕙 *Tue.–Sun. 1–4pm, 8.30–11.30pm*

Fish-frying touches the sublime here: the crunchy sardines and the artfully prepared anchovies, which melt in the mouth, bear full comparison with the most highly rated dishes from the south of Spain. The Barkito's chefs also offer an assortment of rice dishes, *suquets* and whiting recipes… all created with simple ingredients. Relaxed atmosphere and friendly welcome.

Vinya Rosa-Magí (50)
Avinguda Sarriá, 17 - 08029 ☎ 93 430 00 41

Ⓜ *Hospital Clínic* **Creative cuisine** 🗆 ●●● ▣ 🕙 *Mon.–Fri. 1.30–4pm, 8.30–11.30pm; Sat. 8.30–11.30pm*

Founded in the 1950s by the Huguet family, still in charge today, this restaurant successfully flies the flag for traditional cooking, albeit slightly reworked in the quest for new flavors and aromas. Sophistication and refinement are the touchstones, and the tables are arranged so that guests can dine in the utmost privacy. The traditional ingredients of Mediterranean cuisine take pride of place, but they are prepared with such a creative spirit that all their flavors are heightened. Particularly remarkable is the selection of hors-d'œuvre concocted by Magí Huguet: clams and winkles with avocado *à la Bourgogne*, *langostinos* (giant king prawns) with dates. The desserts also play their part in this remarkable culinary spectacle, and the *surtido del demonio goloso*, an assortment of delicious pastries, allows everybody to have a taste.

Not forgetting

■ **Yashima (51)** Carrer Josep Tarradellas, 145 - 08029 ☎ 93 419 06 97 Japanese cuisine ●●● 🕙 Mon.–Sat. 1–4.30pm, 8.30–11.30pm; closed public holidays *A good restaurant with a pleasant atmosphere. Impeccable cooking which makes the best of its ingredients.* ■ **Appetitus (52)** Carrer París, 162 - 08037 ☎ 93 419 49 33 classic cuisine ● 🕙 daily 1.30–4.30pm, 8.30–11.30pm *This modern, recently opened restaurant offers a huge range of salads, carpaccios and other light dishes. Ideal for an informal meal in an attractive setting.*

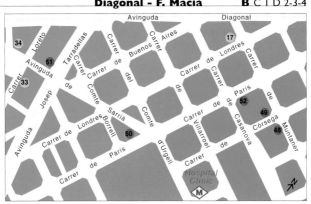

49

52

51

50

The southern half of the neighborhood of Gràcia is a particularly lively area, full of offices and large apartment blocks. The population is extremely varied – a prosperous middle class, Bohemian artists and young people on a tight budget ... and the gastronomic offer is equally

➡ Where to eat

Giardinetto notte (53)
Carrer La Granada del Penedès, 22 - 08006 ☎ 93 218 75 36

Ⓜ *Diagonal* **Classic cuisine** 🍴 ●● ▤ 🍷 Ⓨ *Bar* Mon.–Sat. 1.30–4.30pm, 8.30pm–1am **Restaurant** 1.30–4.30pm, 8.30pm–midnight

The name ('night garden') echoes the restaurant's floral decorations, which pay homage to the famous architect who conceived it in the 1950s. They have never been altered, and now, fifty years on, the place is still blessed with success. The Giardinetto is a classic Barcelona eating-house, its intimacy enhanced by the subdued lighting and the romantic sonatas played on the piano. It is without rival in its preparation of homemade pasta, soups and carpaccios. It has also compiled a wonderful wine list, which concentrates on Catalan labels.

Jean Luc Figueras (54)
Carrer Santa Teresa, 10 - 08012 ☎ 93 415 28 77

Ⓜ *Diagonal* **Creative cuisine** 🍴 ●●●● ▤ 🍷 Mon.–Fri. 1.30–4.30pm, 8.30–11.30pm; Sat. 8.30–11.30pm

This restaurant, on the ground floor of a smart residential building, is indisputably one of the best in town, with high-quality creative cuisine. The sophisticated, elegant but unostentatious setting is matched by expert cooking, rich in subtle combinations: an incursion into the world of haute cuisine which has earned this establishment a reputation without compare. Its *tours de force* include prawns from Palamós in grapefruit vinaigrette, rock fish with tomatoes marinated in oil of Jabugo

diversified, with typical taverns
mingling with luxury
restaurants.

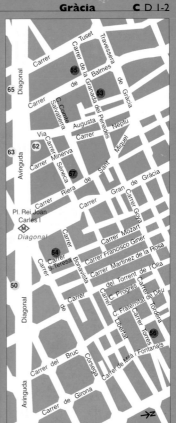

ham and pigeon with black sausage served with soy sauce. Not
forgetting an unsurpassable cheese trolley and a wine list worthy of
close attention.

Flash Flash (55)
Carrer La Granada del Penedés, 25 - 08006 ☎ 93 237 09 90

M *Diagonal* **Creative cuisine** 🍴 ● ▬ 🕐 *daily 1.30–4.30pm,
8.30pm–midnight*

This is the ultimate in fashionable hangouts, where Barcelona's
celebrities come to be seen. Its décor is entirely black and white, lit
by a series of cameras borne by female silhouettes painted on the walls.
The menu is confined to *tortillas* (omelets)… but the choice is virtually
unlimited, from the traditional classics (with potatoes and onions) to
the incredibly extravagant. An unusual experience.

Not forgetting

■ **Ot (56)** Carrer Torres, 25 - 08012 ☎ 93 284 77 52 classic cuisine ●●
🕐 *Mon.–Sat. 1.30–4.30pm, 8.30–11.30pm The first sight of the rundown street
in which this restaurant is tucked away makes it hard to believe that it serves very
classy food. Nevertheless, the Mediterranean specialties, accompanied by carefully
selected wines, are first rate. It is essential to book ahead.* ■ **Roig Robí (57)**
Carrer Seneca, 20 - 08006 ☎ 93 218 92 22 Catalan cuisine ●●● 🕐 *Mon.–Sat.
1.30–4pm, 8.30–11.30pm Elegant and modern restaurant with regional cuisine, in a
setting designed by Antoni Tàpies. Delightful inner courtyard.*

In the area

This smart residential area contains some good restaurants which serve food based on Mediterranean and regional recipes, but prepared with originality and creativity … They rub shoulders with less sophisticated bars offering traditional dishes or tapas.

Where to eat

L'Oliana (58)
Carrer Santaló, 54 - 08021 ☎ 93 201 06 47

🖾 14 *Creative cuisine* 🗂 ●●● 🔲 🕒 *Mon.–Sat. 1–4pm, 8.30pm–midnight; Sun. 1–4pm*

One of the best-known restaurants in the neighborhood, the Oliana produces meticulously and tastefully prepared Mediterranean cuisine, distinguished by the combination of classical inspiration with new flavors and ingredients. The wine list and dessert menu are both varied. The restaurant is large and distributed over several levels opening onto a beautiful inner courtyard. The setting is modern and sophisticated, appropriate for both business lunches and family occasions. The service is attentive and courteous. It is advisable to book ahead, but don't despair if all the tables are occupied: the Oliana sells take-out meals!

El Racó d'en Freixa (59)
Carrer Sant Elíes, 22 - 08021 ☎ 93 209 75 59

🖾 16, 17, 31, 32 *Creative cuisine* ●●●● 🔲 🕒 *Tue.–Sat. 1.30–4.30pm, 8.30–11pm; public holidays 1.30–4.30pm*

The chef who presides over this kitchen is a pioneering figure in local gastronomy, as he is continually exploring new ways of reinventing traditional Catalan cooking. The menu thus contains amazing dishes like tomato in tomatoes, grilled hog fish with mushrooms and snails, and hare stew. The atmosphere is refined, the welcome warm, the service scrupulous … all fully justifying the restaurant's high reputation. Book ahead.

Via Veneto (60)
Carrer Ganduxer, 10 - 08021 ☎ 93 200 72 44

🖾 6, 34 *Creative cuisine* 🗂 ●●●● 🔲 🕒 *Mon.–Fri. 1.30–4.30pm, 8.30–11.30pm; Sat. 8.30–11.30pm*

Elegance, good taste, attention to detail and excellent cooking: these are the touchstones for this highly regarded restaurant. The settings for the various dining-rooms reflect a refined classicism which is matched by the menu. The cuisine, although undeniably drawing on the Mediterranean repertoire, is nonetheless highly elaborate: crab with asparagus, boned guinea fowl, grilled sea bream in vintage wine, and chocolate cake. Let yourself get carried away by the 'special' menu which changes every day so as to give diners a chance to try all the house specialties. There is not only an extensive wine list but also a fine selection of liqueurs and cognacs. It is advisable to book ahead.

Kiyokata (61)
Carrer Muntaner, 231 - 08021 ☎ 93 200 51 26

🖾 58, 64 *Japanese cuisine* ●● 🔲 🕒 *Tue.–Sat. 1.30–4pm, 8.30–11.30pm; Mon. 8.30–11.30pm*

Pleasant atmosphere and thoughtful service, with excellent Japanese cuisine. The set menu at lunchtime (1,500 Ptas) is convenient for those eating in a hurry, while the 'special' menu (4,500 Ptas) reveals the variety of the house specialties.

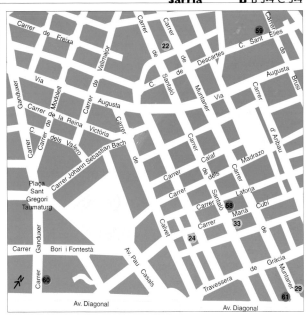

58

59

61

In the area

This wealthy neighborhood, checkered with the gardens of villas and apartment buildings, does not abound in shops or restaurants! However, the menus of some restaurants are particularly varied, and suited to every appetite and budget.

Where to eat

Neichel (62)
Carrer Beltràn y Rózpide 16bis - 08034 ☎ 93 203 84 08

▦ 63,78 **Creative cuisine** 🔲 ●●●● ▭ 🕒 *Mon.–Fri. 1.30–4.30pm, 8.30–11.30pm; Sat. 8.30–11.30pm*

This is a highly prestigious restaurant, whose menu is imbued with imagination and seeks to attain perfection every day. The chef brilliantly adapts the French culinary tradition to local produce and concocts some extremely spectacular and elaborate dishes. Particularly to be recommended are the duck carpaccios, the artichokes in vinaigrette of truffles, the John Dory with *croûtons* and cream of sea urchins, the spicy crunches and the *mató* (a kind of solid yogurt) ice cream with lavender honey. Not to mention the exceptionally well stocked cheese trolley and the wine list, with 300 different labels. It is advisable to book ahead.

Triton (63)
Carrer Alfambra, 16 - 08034 ☎ 93 203 30 85

Ⓜ *Zona Universitaria* **Classic cuisine** 🔲 ●●● ▭ 🕒 *Mon.–Sat. 1.30–4.30pm, 8.30–11.30pm; closed public holidays*

This establishment provides the best quality/price ratio in Pedralbes, together with the certainty of eating quickly and informally. The atmosphere is pleasant, and the menu offers simple tasty dishes based on natural seasonal produce.

Paradis Barcelona (64)
Passeig Manuel Girona, 7 - 08034 ☎ 93 203 76 37

▦ 63, 78 **Classic cuisine** 🔲 ● ▭ 🕒 *Mon.–Sat. 1.30–4.30pm, 8.30–11.30pm; Sun. 1.30–4.30pm*

This is the headquarters of a major restaurant chain, which also sells take-out food. It caters for family groups, as well as organizing receptions and banquets. Customers with healthy appetites love to take advantage of the free buffet, which is available both at lunch and at dinner: for a set price, which may vary according to the dishes on offer (2,000–2,500 Ptas, not including drinks), they can try all the specialties and come back for more as often as they like! The tables are almost overflowing with hors-d'œuvre, hot and cold appetizers, fish and meat dishes, cakes, tarts, mousses and other delicacies. A feast for the eyes – and the taste buds!

Sal i Pebre (65)
Carrer Alfambra, 14 - 08034 ☎ 93 205 36 58

Ⓜ *Zona Universitaria* **Classic cuisine** 🔲 ●● ▭ 🕒 *daily 1.30–4.30pm, 8.30–11.30pm*

The home cooking, rooted in the Mediterranean tradition, is top-quality here, and the prices are reasonable. The dishes are light, and emphasize their natural and fresh ingredients. Sal i Pebre also offers a set menu at lunchtime.

Carrer d' Alfambra
65 63

Avinguda

Carrer Tinet

Carrer Jordi Girona

Palau Reial
M Diagonal
53

65

de Pedralbes
Carrer Beltran Ròzpide
64 Passeig

62 62

25 Plaça de Pius XII
Avinguda
Carrer Jimenez Iglesias

62

63

C. del Dr. Ferran

Manuel Girona

Maria Cristina
M
Plaça de la Reina Maria Cristina
Carrer del Capità Arenas

Avinguda Diagonal

Gran Via de Carles III

N

64 62

In the area

The Tibidabo hill, the highest in Barcelona, provides the setting for elegant residential neighborhoods dotted with green areas and aristocratic mansions. The basilica and fairground on its peak are popular with the locals in the evenings and on weekends, so it is not surprising

Where to eat

El Asador de Aranda (66)
Avinguda del Tibidabo, 31 - 08022 ☎ 93 417 01 15

🚌 58, 75, 85 + tramvia blau *Regional cuisine* ●● 🔲 🕐 *Mon.–Sat. 1.30–4.30pm, 8.30pm–midnight; Sun. 1.30–4.30pm*

The Asador, as it is known for short, is housed in a splendid listed building – la Casa Roviralta – which boasts a successful marriage of traditional Castilian gastronomy and Catalan Modernist architecture. The interior decoration takes full advantage of the building's resources: the various rooms, each with its own individual character, have been converted into either spacious banqueting halls for large groups, or more intimate areas for smaller parties. Be sure to explore every nook and cranny of this labyrinth, and do not overlook the delightful garden. The menu concentrates on meat dishes, such as roast lamb – one of the specialties of Catalan cooking – cooked to perfection, although there is also some excellent delicatessen … Every appetite will be satisfied here, as the portions are truly generous.

La Venta (67)
Plaça Doctor Andreu, s/n - 08035 ☎ 93 212 64 55

🚌 b 58, 75, 85 + tramvia blau *Catalan cuisine* 🔳 ●●● 🔲 🕐 *Mon.–Sat. 1.30–4.30pm, 8.30–11.30pm* 🌿

Perched on the Tibidabo hill, this restaurant affords an extraordinary panoramic view of Barcelona, and in fine weather its customers can also take advantage of the pleasant terrace. The décor in this old bar mixes colonial-style elements with features borrowed from the coastal towns. Catalan specialties prepared with care, without any frills, excellent desserts and a fine wine list.

La Balsa (68)
Carrer Infanta Isabel, s/n 08022 ☎ 93 211 50 48

🚌 64, 73, then short taxi ride *Catalan cuisine* 🔳 ●●● 🔲 🕐 *Mon.–Sat. 1.30–4.30pm, 8.30pm–midnight* ⭐ 🌿

This restaurant, nestling idyllically amid sheltering greenery, is held in particularly high esteem on account of its both peacefulness and its warm and inviting décor, based on wood and glass (large bay windows). This decoration has rightly won it the top prize of FAD (Spanish Federation of Architects and Designers). The garden/terrace, which provides a panoramic view of Barcelona, is very attractive, especially when the temperatures soar downtown … meals are served there, in the shadows of lush and fragrant vegetation. The food is equally striking, with a classical repertoire imbued in the Catalan tradition, yet marked by inventiveness and modernity. Do not miss the excellent homemade goose paté, which can be eaten as either a starter or a main course.

that a number
of bars and
restaurants have
sprung up.

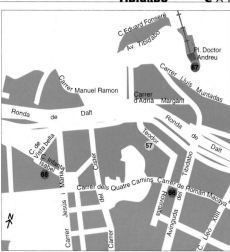

The Tibidabo hill
overlooking the city
boasts a number of
restaurants serving tasty
Catalan dishes.

Spanish pork products have a world-wide reputation, and their crowning achievement is *jamón* (ham), whether *serrano* (cured), *ibérico* (from black pigs) or *jabugo* (from the town of Jabugo) This tradition inspires great respect in Catalonia, and it is the basis of the menu in many bars. Do not forget to accompany your snacks with a traditional *pa amb tomaquet*

 # Where to eat

69

El Mesón Cinco Jotas (69)
Rambla de Catalunya, 91/93 - 08008 ☎ 93 487 91 21

Ⓜ *Passeig de Gràcia* ● ▤ Ⓥ *daily 1–11.30pm*

In Spain everybody knows that Cinco Jotas is synonymous with top-quality ham. Its founder, Sanchez Romero Carvajal, first made his name in 1979 with his succulent *jabugo*, and quickly went on to win a string of official awards and make his 'five J' brand popular with an ever-growing public. Today this restaurant belongs to a chain which uses his brand-name to sell its wares. Here there is a great array of hams and sausages, but there are also some fine gourmet cheeses for discerning palates. A good spot for an informal cold meal.

El Rincón del Jamón (70)
Carrer Salvador Espriu, 23 - 08005 ☎ 93 221 77 55

Ⓜ *Ciutadella* ● ▤ Ⓥ *daily 1–11.30pm* 🚇 *Avinguda Diagonal, 557 - 08019 in the Illa shopping mall, n° 2–27* ☎ 934440134 Ⓜ *María Cristina* ● ▤ Ⓥ *Daily 9am–11.30pm*

The chain of Rincón del Jamón restaurants owes its success to the quality of its products. Their sausages, and their delicatessen in general – from the *morcilla* (blood pudding) and *longaniza* (long sausage) to the *panceta* (smoked tripe) – are particularly worthy of note, but their wide selection of hams and huge assortment of tapas should not be neglected. The atmosphere is informal and the position strategic: near the big Illa shopping mall and the Olympic Village, the Rincón is right in the heart of the new Barcelona, in areas buzzing with life.

(toasted bread rubbed with tomato and sprinkled with salt and olive oil).

Casa Alfonso (71)
Carrer Roger de Llúria, 6 - 08010 ☎ 93 200 51 26

M *Passeig de Gràcia* ● ▣ 🖸 *Mon.–Fri. 1.30–4.30pm, 8.30–11.30pm; Sat. 8.30–11.30pm*

This restaurant serves excellent home cooking at reasonable prices … and the best delicatessen in Spain. Here you will find not only the great Catalan specialties – *butifarras* (white or black sausages), *cansaladas* (tripe), *llangonises* (long sausages) and *bulls* (liver sausages), all served with the traditional *pa amb tomaquet* – but also the *morcillas* (blood puddings) and *chorizos* from other parts of Spain. And, of course, ham – *ibérico* or *serrano* – accompanied by a host of regional cheeses and homemade pâtés. A family atmosphere, always very cheerful.

El Drapaire (72)
Carrer Sitges, 11 - 08002 ☎ 93 302 76 28

M *Catalunya* ●● ▣ 🖸 *Tue.–Sun. 5.30pm–2.30am*

A typical eatery, with rustic décor – old wooden tables in an alarmingly small room – always full of people and smoke. The mainly young clientele is particularly attracted by the quality/price ratio of the excellent delicatessen and the Catalan specialties, all washed down with fine wines …

63

Café Internet

One of the places most appreciated by travelers tired of struggling with a foreign language: here they can use their own once again, and spend an evening surfing the Internet. *Gran Vía de les Corts Catalanes, 656 - 08010 ☎ 933021154* *Passeig de Gràcia ● 500 500 Ptas per session*

After dar

Fitness

Sporty travelers can choose from a wide range of fitness centers open to non-members, even if they are only in town for a few days. The gymnasiums belonging to the DIR chain are recommended. The most recent addition is not far from the Diagonal: *Carrer Ganduxer, 25/27 - 08021 ☎ 932016031 ● up to 1,000 Ptas per day.*

Open-air bars

Barcelona's remarkably mild climate, even in winter, has given rise to a host of *terrasses*, bars with outdoor tables which are available all the year round. The most famous ones are scattered along the Ramblas, or under the arches of the Plaça Reial. However, do not overlook the Zurich on the corner of Plaça Catalunya and Carrer Pelai, or the bars and restaurants in the port, in Maremagnum and in Barcelona, up to the Olympic port. For those who do not fancy braving the sea breeze, they all have efficient heating systems inside!

'Guía del Ocio' and 'La Agenda de Barcelona'

Indispensable equipment for anybody who wants to make the most of Barcelona's resources, these two weekly pocket guides list the movies, theater shows, concerts, exhibitions and other attractions which liven up the city by day and by night.

41 Nights out

THE INSIDER'S FAVORITES

Barcelona is one of Europe's music capitals. Music enthusiasts closely follow the operatic and orchestral seasons, and enjoy the work of Catalan composers as much as Italian and German ones. Catalonia has always been a nursery for great lyric singers, and some of its best exponents, such as Montserrat Caballé, Victoria de los Angeles and

After dark

Gran Teatre del Liceu (1)
La Rambla, 55 - 08002 ☎ 93 485 99 00

Ⓜ *Liceu Oct.–July* 🕐 *Box office Mon.–Fri. 2pm–8.30pm; Sat., Sun. open one hour before performance* ● *1,000–20,000 Ptas*

Built in 1638, after a design by Miquel Garriga i Roca, the Liceu is one of the most famous theaters in the world and one of the leaders in Europe as regards acoustics and capacity. A terrible fire in 1994, the second in its history, has deprived the city of one of its most prestigious institutions … but it has made possible the construction, in record time, of a new ultra-modern auditorium, equipped with all the latest technology. The Liceu has always presented top-class operas and ballets performed by international stars (and will continue to do so once reopened). Since the 1994 fire, an association of music lovers meets in front of the theater, every Saturday at noon, to give small-scale open air concerts.

Palau de la Música (2)
Carrer Amadeu Vives, 1 - 08038 ☎ 93 268 10 00

Ⓜ *Season September–May (operatic and orchestral music); September–July (pop and jazz)* 🕐 *Box office daily 10am–one hour before concert Concerts every night (varying times) and Sunday mornings* ● *800-20,000 Ptas*

Although initially subject to fierce criticism and heated debate, this building is now universally recognized as one of the most beautiful examples of Modernist architecture in Barcelona. Built in 1908 by Domènech i Montaner, the building was decorated in accordance with the purest principles of Art Nouveau. Mainly known for its orchestral concerts, since the Liceu fire the Palau de la Música has also put on lyric recitals and a few operas. It also organizes concerts of jazz, pop and traditional Spanish music.

Auditori (3)
Carrer Lepant ang. Ausias Marc, s/n - 08013 ☎ 93 247 93 00

Ⓜ *Season September–July* 🕐 *Box office daily 10am–9pm Concerts every night (varying times)* ● *1,000–20,000 Ptas*

The city's latest music center, the work of the architect Rafael Moneo, contains one large concert hall, with a capacity for 2,300 people, and a smaller multi-purpose space, equipped with mobile seating for 700 spectators. It faces the National Theater of Catalonia, and since March 1999 it has filled out the already long list of venues for orchestral music and opera in Barcelona, although it does not neglect other genres, and has already put on concerts of flamenco, jazz and African music …

Teatre Victoria (4)
Avinguda del Paral.lel, 67 - 08001 ☎ 93 443 29 29

Ⓜ *Paral.lel Season September–mid-July* 🕐 *Performances Tue.–Sun. Box office Tue.–Sun. 5pm–one hour before the performance* ● *1,500–3,500 Ptas*

A theater from the 1960s which has recently been refurbished. The large dimensions of its auditorium means that it traditionally houses large musical shows, such as those of the Dagoll Dagom company. Since the Liceu fire it has also put on the main productions of Barcelona's operatic season.

José Carreras, are now part of
the international elite.

Opera and classical music

In Barcelona, culture is inextricably linked with nationalistic issues and has always played a leading role in the life of the city ... and dramatic art has traditionally been predominant. The evidence for this lies in the countless plays presented every day, either in Catalan or in Spanish, without mentioning performances by foreign companies or the host of

After dark

Teatre Nacional de Catalunya (5)
Plaça de les Arts, I - 08013 ☎ 93 306 57 06

Ⓜ *Glòries Season September–July* 🕔 **Box office** *Tue.–Sun. noon–8pm*
Performances *Tue.–Sat. 9pm; Sun. 6pm* ● *2,600–3,000 Ptas*

The building which houses the National Theater of Catalonia, opened in 1997, is the brainchild of the Catalan architect Ricardo Bofill. This huge Parthenon contains three auditoria of various sizes and can thus accommodate several shows at the same time: the smaller stages are given over to experimental contemporary productions by regional companies or plays by emerging writers. It also puts on classical works, and the productions are generally of a high standard. Puppet shows are also occasionally presented, and once a year a lyric opera is staged (*Calisto* by Cavalli in 1997–98, *Alcina* by Handel in 1998–99).

Poliorama (6)
La Rambla, 115 - 08002 ☎ 93 318 81 81

Ⓜ *Catalunya Season September–July* 🕔 **Box office** *Tue.–Sat. 5–8pm; Sun. 5–6pm* **Performances** *varying times* ● *2,000–3,500 Ptas*

The Poliorama occupies a symbolic place in Catalan theater and is often chosen by leading directors and local companies for their premieres. Thus, Mario Gas, Josep Maria Flotats, el Tricicle and T de Teatre, to name just a few, have all opened new works here. The theater also regularly serves as a venue for Catalan singer-songwriters like Lluís Llach, Maria del Mar Bonet and Marina Rosell.

Tivoli (7)
Carrer Casp, 8 - 08010 ☎ 93 412 20 63

Ⓜ *Catalunya Season January–December* 🕔 **Box office** *Tue.–Sun. 11.30am–2pm, 4.30–8pm* **Performances** *varying times* ● *2,000–4,000 Ptas*

This theater is an institution of the Barcelona theater world. Its program is varied: dance, concerts, *zarzuela* (a kind of Spanish operetta), plays and even circus.

Sala Muntaner (8)
Carrer Muntaner, 4 - 08011 ☎ 93 451 57 52

Ⓜ *Universitat Seasons September–July* 🕔 **Box office** *I hour before the performance* **Performances** *Wed.–Sun. 9pm, 10.30pm* ● *Wed., Thu. 1,500 Ptas; Fri.–Sun. 2,000 Ptas*

Small fringe theater, a frequent venue for young performers or little-known companies putting on new or alternative shows.

Teatre Principal (9)
La Rambla, 27 - 08002 ☎ 93 301 47 50

Ⓜ *Drassanes Season September–July* 🕔 **Box office** *2 hours before the performance* **Performances** *Tue., Wed., Fri. 10pm; Thu. 6pm, 10pm; Sat. 6.30pm, 10.30 pm; Sun 6pm* ● *variable*

A theater with a long history, which specialized in movie screenings until 1997. Its program includes cabaret and music-hall shows.

musicals on offer.

Places for watching flamenco dancing are normally small, smoky and crowded. The reduced dimensions of the *tablao*, or stage, allow the audience to be in close contact with the musicians and dancers … and feel the soul and intensity of the flamenco. Do not think that these places only exist for the benefit of tourists: there are just as many

After dark

Los Tarantos (10)
Plaça Reial, 17 - 08002 ☎ 93 318 30 67

Ⓜ *Liceu* Ⓞ *Performances Mon.–Sat. 10pm* **Discotheque** *Mon.–Sat. 2–5am* ● *3,800 Ptas* Ⓨ Ⓞ Ⓕ

Los Tarantos, one of the main showcases for flamenco in Barcelona, nestles under the arches of the wonderful Plaça Reial, and many big names in Spanish flamenco have performed on its *tablao*. After 2am the place changes its function and the atmosphere is transformed: the strident singing and stirring choreography of flamenco give way to the boisterous rhythms of salsa, merengue and rumba. The emphasis is on world music.

Los Juaneles (11)
Carrer Aldana, 4 - 08015

Ⓜ *Paral.lel* Ⓞ *Tue., Thu. from 9pm to the last customer; Fri., Sat. from 10.30pm to the last customer* ● *admission free* Ⓟ Ⓨ Ⓕ

The purity of flamenco's style means that it makes no concessions to folklore, and this venue is strictly for enlightened fans. On Thursday evenings, the atmosphere is completely different, as there are *sevillana* classes, open to all … a great time is guaranteed, even if you do not regularly practice traditional Spanish dancing! You will find it very difficult to stay in your seat when confronted with the array of colors and rhythms unfurling before your eyes. On Thursdays you can also try some reasonably priced Andalusian specialties, and you are obliged to buy a drink.

Tablao de Carmen (12)
Arcs, 9 - 08038 (inside the Poble Espanyol) ☎ 93 325 68 95

Ⓜ *Plaça d'Espanya* Ⓑ *13,61* Ⓞ *Tue.–Sun. 8pm–1am* **Performances** *two per night: 9.30pm, 11.30pm (Fri., Sat. 9.30pm, midnight)* ● *from 4,200 Ptas to 7,200 Ptas* Ⓟ Ⓨ Ⓕ

Its location, in the Andalusian section of the Spanish village ➡ 98 makes it the one venue in the whole of Barcelona which most faithfully recreates the art of flamenco and the atmosphere of a *tablao*. Large groups frequently visit and it is often packed … so it is better to book ahead. There is no door charge, but there is an obligatory drink (4,200 Ptas). Budget for 7,200 Ptas to have dinner.

Patio Andaluz (13)
Carrer Aribau, 242 - 08006 ☎ 93 209 33 78

Ⓜ *Diagonal* Ⓞ *Daily 8pm–4am* **Performances** *two per night: daily 10pm, 12.45am* ● *from 4,000 Ptas* Ⓟ Ⓨ Ⓕ

A venue very popular with foreigners attracted by Spanish folklore. Its audience consists almost entirely of the uninitiated … and it shows in the flamenco on offer. Nevertheless, the shows are extremely colorful and manage to win over both those who are discovering the art of flamenco for the first time and those who are already familiar with it. The restaurant has set menus which concentrate on traditional dishes from the south of Spain.

knowledgeable locals, immersed in the secrets and techniques of this ancient dance.

10

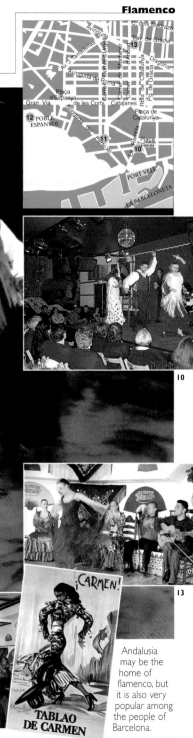

10

13

13

¡CARMEN!

TABLAO DE CARMEN

Andalusia may be the home of flamenco, but it is also very popular among the people of Barcelona.

In the 19th century Barcelona's artists and intellectuals loved to meet in cafés to indulge in passionate heated discussions, which often lasted all night. Some of these cafés still exist, and have managed to maintain their character, and it is very enjoyable to drop in and quietly savor a slice of Barcelona life.

After dark

El Café de la Ópera (14)
La Rambla, 74 - 08002 ☎ 93 302 41 80

Ⓜ *Liceu* 🕐 *daily 9am–2am* ● *admission free* 🍸

One of the few authentic cafés remaining in Barcelona, which explains the constant stream of people passing through, at all times of the day, seven days a week ... A traditional meeting place and the site of interminable *tertulias* (group debates) among intellectuals and artists. Despite its popularity, the atmosphere is subdued, and some customers even bring a book along to read. When the weather is good, you can sit at the tables set outside under a canopy, on the Rambla, facing the Liceu opera house which gives the café its name.

La Taverneta (15)
Passatge Duc de la Victoria, 3 - 08002 ☎ 93 302 61 52

Ⓜ *Catalunya, Liceu* 🕐 *daily 1pm–4pm, 7pm–2am* ● *admission free* 🍴 🍸 🎵

At mealtimes this is an excellent restaurant which serves tasty dishes at extremely reasonable prices. At nights the Taverneta reveals its Bohemian spirit; any customer who fancies livening the place up with a song will find a guitar to use as accompaniment, and an enthusiastic and good-natured audience ... For thirty years the owners of the Taverneta have provided a friendly welcome for their clientele, and have managed to keep it entertained with original pastimes, such as Tarot readings.

Els Quatre Gats (16)
Carrer Montsió, 3 - 08002 ☎ 93 302 41 40

Ⓜ *Catalunya* 🕐 *daily 8am–2am* ● *admission free* 🍴 🍸

Obviously based on the Chat-Noir, the famous satirical cabaret in Montmartre, this café was already famous when Picasso lived in Barcelona – he even designed the menu – and is still used for artistic and literary get-togethers. During the dictatorship, when it was dangerous to publicly express disapproval of the regime, a great many political meetings were held here. The café also offers a restaurant service (set menus at lunchtime). Its walls are decorated with portraits of its most famous customers, along with works by Catalan artists from the turn of the century, and these blend in perfectly with the Modernist furniture. It is especially appealing in the afternoon, when Els Quatre Gats becomes a quiet, intimate bar, where one can enjoy a book in peace, sipping from a cup of good coffee. For lovers of spots imbued with history.

Not forgetting

■ **Velódromo (17)** Carrer Muntaner, 213 - 08036 ☎ 93 430 60 22 🕐 *Mon.–Sat. 6am–2am This place has managed to maintain its atmosphere of an old-style café. Elegant tables and a pool room.*
■ **Café del Sol (18)** Plaça del Sol, 16 - 08012 ☎ 93 415 56 63 🕐 *daily noon–2am In the heart of the Gràcia neighborhood, the Café del Sol has an excellent pianist, who has greatly contributed to its popularity. Exhibitions of paintings and photographs are regularly held here.*

The legendary Café de la Ópera and Els Quatre Gats played an important role in the cultural and artistic life of 19th-century Barcelona.

73

In the 1980s, Barcelona lived through a period of feverish creativity. Top architects and interior decorators designed some revolutionary nightspots, in which the latest materials and building techniques brought hi-tech to the fore. Barcelona has thus become an international reference point in this field. These days there are still certain bars which

After dark

Nick Havanna – the ultimate bar (19)
Carrer Rosselló, 208 - 08008 ☎ 93 215 65 91

Ⓜ *Diagonal* 🕐 *Sun.–Thu. 11pm–4am; Fri., Sat. 11pm–5am* ● *Sun.–Thu. admission free; Fri., Sat. 1,100 Ptas* 🍸 🎵

A bar which symbolizes Barcelona's nightlife, this space, with its revolutionary architecture which seems to withstand passing trends, has become an enduring classic. The enormous pendulum which swings unsettlingly above the dance floor has only added to its fame. The live music here embraces all styles of music: pop-rock, funk, techno or salsa … Parties are often organized round a theme, sometimes even to promote a new drink. This bar is recommended from Thursday to Saturday for those who like mingling with a crowd.

Schilling (20)
Carrer Ferran, 23 - 08002 ☎ 93 317 67 87

Ⓜ *Liceu* 🕐 *daily 10am–2.30am* ● *admission free* 🍸

An old cutler's shop converted into a trendy bar, the Schilling has become an institution in the old city, and is almost exclusively frequented by people from the fashion world. Its décor has won it appearances in several advertisements. It often exhibits works by young, often unknown, artists, displayed in small showcases which echo the shape of the large bay windows. Regulars position themselves at these windows to get a good view of the street … and to be seen.

Margarita Blue (21)
Carrer Josep Anselm Clavé, 6 - 08022 ☎ 93 317 71 76

Ⓜ *Drassanes* 🕐 *daily 10.30am–2am* 🍴 🍸 🎵 ● *admission free*

Tex-mex cuisine and cocktails replete with fantasy (including the explosive Margarita Blue which gives this café its name) have turned this into one of the favorite haunts of Barcelona's in-crowd. The design by Agata Ruíz de la Prada, with its mix of modern lamps and furniture and unusual recycled objects, gives this old customs office a unique atmosphere. Small-scale theatrical events and other performances are often put on here.

Not forgetting

■ **Zig Zag (22)** Carrer Plató, 13 - 08006 ☎ 93 201 62 07 🕐 *daily 10pm–3am One of Barcelona's most fashionable nightspots in the uptown district. House music and funk have pride of place.*
■ **Bosc de les fades (23)** Passatge de la Banca, 7 - 08002 ☎ 93 317 26 49 🕐 *daily 10am–1am, Fri., Sat. 10am–2am Café situated next to the Wax Museum, which owes its special atmosphere to the fortune tellers who read cards for the customers. Book presentations and small-scale concerts.*
■ **Más y más (24)** Carrer Marià Cubí, 199 - 08021 ☎ 93 209 45 02 🕐 *daily 7pm–3am One of the places where the Barcelona nightlife is at its most intense.*

lead the way in the city's night-time entertainment.

A visit to the city's designer bars is a must if you want to have your finger on the pulse and experience Barcelona's latest trends.

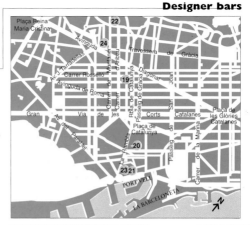

75

Any survey of Barcelona's nightlife would be incomplete without mentioning its jazz clubs, which put on high-quality concerts all year round. However, their programs come to a peak with the summer festival (June–July). A word of warning: although in fine weather the street is generally the main arena for performances in Barcelona, jazz

After dark

Harlem Jazz Club (25)
Carrer Comtessa de Sobradiel, 8 - 08002 ☎ 93 310 07 55

M *Liceu* ◐ *Sun.–Thu. 8pm–4am* **Performances** *8pm, midnight* ● *admission free* ▧ ♬

Very lively club with an extremely knowledgeable clientele from all over the world, united by their passion for jazz. These connoisseurs have the chance to enjoy at close range the work of major international musicians, as well as the most important Spanish groups.

Jamboree (26)
Plaça Reial, 17 - 08002 ☎ 93 301 75 64

M *Liceu* ◐ *daily midnight–4am* ● *1,500 Ptas* ▧ ◉ ♬

This famous nightspot, which has made an enormous contribution to the history of Spanish jazz, offers live music until 2am. After that the Jamboree is transformed into a discotheque specializing in rap, funk and African music. This club is tucked under the beautiful arches of the Plaça Reial, a favorite meeting place for young travelers passing through Barcelona.

Pipa Club Jazz - Robin Hood (27)
Rambla Santa Mònica, 31 - 08002 ☎ 93 301 88 81

M *Liceu -* ◐ *Sun.–Thu. 11pm–1am, Fri., Sat. 11.30pm–1.30am* ● *1,000 Ptas; admission free for members of Barcelona Pipa Club* ▧ ♬

The traditional Barcelona Pipa Club, one of the temples of jazz in Barcelona, renowned for its laid-back atmosphere and the high quality of its concerts, has decided to open a second venue, on account of the overwhelming demand. It opened in March 1999 with a concert by Albert Bonver, the top pianist from the old club: the Robin Hood is sure to maintain the high standards of its big brother!

Bar Pastis (28)
Rambla Santa Mónica, 4 - 08002 ☎ 93 318 79 80

M *Drassanes* ◐ *daily 7.30pm–2.30am* ● *admission free* ▧ ♬

A bar in the old city soaked in history, in a neighborhood full of charm. Only 20 tables and 8 barstools fit into this tiny place, which the owner, a colorful character who quit his philosophy degree to run the bar, has decided to dedicate to the French songs of the early years of the century, particularly the repertoire of Edith Piaf and Jacques Brel. You might be lucky enough to chance on a live performance – they are fairly frequent, but not really planned in advance!

Not forgetting

■ **Luz de Gas (29)** Carrer Muntaner, 246 - 08021 ☎ 93 209 77 11 ◐ *daily midnight–3am This 'theater-club' puts on jazz and country music concerts, and also operas, in a Belle Époque cabaret setting.*

■ **La Boîte (30)** Avinguda Diagonal, 477 - 08006 ☎ 93 419 59 50 ◐ *daily 11pm–5.30am Charming nightspot popular with musicians and artists in search of an intimate atmosphere. Live concerts every night.*

events are more likely to take
place behind closed doors.

27

26

Games, drinks, cocktails, infusions, culture and music: these are the main ingredients of Barcelona's cocktail bars. From Boadas, the oldest and classiest, to more recent arrivals, there is an unrivaled choice of places to celebrate the essential ritual of the aperitif, which in Barcelona, a city where the timetable always has an element of fantasy,

After dark

Boadas (31)
Carrer Tallers, I - 08001 ☎ 93 318 95 92

🅜 Catalunya 🕓 Sun.–Thu. noon–2am ● admission free 🍸

The cocktail bar par excellence: it attracts a crowd which defies all attempts at classification, from artists and intellectuals drawn by the traditional, expertly prepared alcoholic mixes to business people making deals and politicians in meetings which may have a decisive impact on the life of the city. Paradoxically, it is the small size – and hence its lack of tables – which gives Boadas its charm. The bar acquires even more vitality and intensity with its customers perched on high stools and clustered around the bar.

Dry Martini (32)
Carrer Aribau, 166 - 08036 ☎ 93 217 50 72

🅜 Diagonal 🚌 54 🕓 daily 6.30pm–2.30am, Fri., Sat. 6.30pm–3am ● admission free 🍸

Javier de las Muelas, one of Barcelona's top barmen, knows how to create delicious cocktails through masterly combinations of ingredients. The walls of the bar are covered in posters extolling the virtues of Martini. A back room has just been turned into the only speakeasy in town, a replica of the clandestine bars in the Chicago of the 1930s, the legendary Prohibition era.

Gimlet (33)
Carrer Santaló, 46 - 08021 ☎ 93 201 53 06

🅜 Fontana 🕓 Sun.–Thu. 7pm–2.30am, Fri., Sat. 7pm–3am ● admission free 🍸
🚇 Carrer Rec, 24 - 08003 ☎ 93 310 10 27 🅜 Jaume I 🕓 7pm–3am ● admission free 🍸

Excellent bar which boasts that it offers the best cocktails in town … and one can see why it has christened itself after the favorite drink of the private eye Philip Marlowe. The branch in Carrer Santaló has large comfortable tables, while the more austere one in Carrer Rec only has bar stools. The former attracts a young crowd, while the latter, in the heart of the Ribera, has been 'colonized' by artists and intellectuals.

El Paraigua (34)
Carrer Pas de l'Ensenyança, 2 - 08002 ☎ 93 217 50 72

🅜 Jaume I 🕓 daily 6pm–2.30am ● admission free 🍸

A very appealing Modernist bar, with two floors: on the first, a café with a restful atmosphere and classical music in the background; on the second a bar renowned for its cocktails and whiskies.

Not forgetting

■ **Oliver & Hardy (35)** Avinguda Diagonal, 593 (interno) - 08021 ☎ 93 419 31 81 🕓 daily 8.35pm–5am *Chic piano bar next to the Hilton, with a restaurant and discotheque. Live music at midnight on Wednesdays.*
■ **Ideal (36)** Carrer Aribau, 89 - 08036 ☎ 93 453 10 28 🕓 daily 7pm–2am *The atmosphere in this luxury cocktail bar is typical of Barcelona.*

can be taken at any time of the day or night.

31

There is no telling people's tastes, but Barcelona has something to satisfy even the most demanding night owl. A wealth of discotheques, a huge range of musical styles (revival, electronic music, Latin rhythms …) and, above all, unrestricted opening hours. If you want to finish partying in daylight, you can be sure that you will always find somewhere to go: in

After dark

Otto Zutz (37)
Carrer Lincoln, 15 - 08006 ☎ 93 238 07 22

M *Gràcia* ⊙ *Tue.–Sat. 8pm–5am* ● *from 2,000 Ptas* 📶 ◎ ♫

Fashionable discotheque which offers its clientele of top models and show-business celebrities three very different areas, spread over three floors. The first is given over to techno, the second aims to please those with a nostalgia for the 1960s and 1970s, while the third is strictly reserved for VIPs. Every Wednesday there is a chance to have dinner (having previously booked ahead) while watching a show (a live concert or magic show).

Up & Down (38)
Carrer Numancia, 179 - 08034 ☎ 93 205 51 94

M *Maria Cristina* ⊙ *Tue.–Sat. midnight–4am* 🍴 📶 ◎ ♫ *Up* ● *2,000 Ptas* 👔 *jacket obligatory* **Down** ● *2,000 Ptas*

A name which not only reflects the venue's two different spaces but also sums up the fortunes of this nightclub over the last few years: busy phases alternating with periods of oblivion! These days it is successful once more, chiefly as a result of the 'Down' Wednesdays devoted to *sevillanas*, and its 'Down light' programs at the beginning of the evening (6–9pm) on Fridays and Saturdays. Soon there will also be a restaurant serving lunch and dinner.

Nayandei (39)
Moll d'Espanya, Port Vell (inside the Maremagnum commercial center, loc. 204-205) - 08003 ☎ 93 225 80 10

M *Drassanes, Barceloneta* ⊙ *daily 9pm–5am* ● *admission free* 📶 ◎ ♫ ✖ ⛷

This is the most popular nightspot on Barcelona's seafront, and is greatly enhanced by an immense terrace of 10,700 sq. ft on the roof of Maremagnum, a special treat in hot weather. Carlo Martínez, the designer of this huge discotheque, has dreamed up two spaces with completely different atmospheres: one, with warm colors, evokes the day, while the other, with its dark colors and starry ceiling, the night.

Bikini (40)
Carrer Deu i Mata, 105 - 08025 ☎ 93 322 08 00

M *Les Corts* ⊙ *daily 11.30pm–5am* ● *Mon.–Wed. admission free; Thu. 1,000 Ptas; Fri.–Sun. 1,500 Ptas* ◎

The legendary Bikini has recently reopened in a brand new building on its former site. Three spaces provide a wide choice of music; the one devoted to Latin rhythms is often graced by dance teachers who teach customers the more difficult steps … go on, don't doubt your ability!

Sala Metro (41)
Carrer Sepúlveda, 185 - 08011 ☎ 93 323 52 27

M *Universitat* ⊙ *daily midnight–5am* ● *1,000 Ptas* ◎

The first and best-known gay discotheque in Barcelona. It manages to satisfy varying musical tastes with two spaces: one for the latest sounds, the other for fans of earlier periods.

fact, some venues only open their doors from 7am to noon …

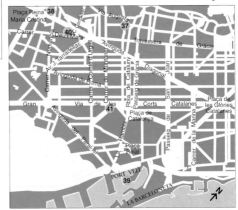

Since the 1980s Barcelona nightlife has been on a par with any of Europe's great capital cities.

Touring the city in a double-decker

The **Bus Turístic** offers 2 trips around town, from March to January 6. There are 24 stops, which allow passengers to see all the main sights.
- 1 day 1,700 Ptas; 2 days 2,300 Ptas

What to see

On the trail of Modernism

This **Ruta del Modernisme**, a guided thematic tour, explores the buildings most characteristic of 19th-century Barcelona.
☎ 90 210 12 12
- 1,500/900 Ptas; tickets on sale at the Palau Güell and the Casa Lleó Morera.

Pass for museums and public transport

The Barcelona Card, on sale in tourist offices, provides free access to public transport and reduced admission charges in some museums (Barbier-Mueller, MACBA, CCCB, Espai Gaudí, Fundació Miró, Fundació Tàpies, Thyssen-Bornemisza).

● 24 hr, 2,500/2,000 Ptas; 48 hr, 3,000/2,500 Ptas; 72 hr, 3,500/3,000 Ptas

58
Sights
THE INSIDER'S FAVORITES

INDEX BY SUBJECT

Postcards from Barcelona: the Rambla, the 'backbone' of the city, is busy day and night (1); the Casa Batlló (2) an outstanding example of Gaudí's work; the bold structures of the Olympic Port display the new face of modern Barcelona (3); the skyscrapers and whale by Gehry in the Olympic Village (4); a corner in the city's medieval Barri Gòtic (5); 'Dona

➡ **What to see**

2

Barcelona is endowed with a historical legacy which rivals that of any other great European capital. Although proud of its Roman past, its golden age spanned the 13th and 15th centuries, reflecting the advent of Catalonian expansionism in the Mediterranean. The imposing medieval monuments in the Barri Gòtic bear witness to this period of prosperity ➡86. The discovery of the Americas – with which the Catalans were forbidden to trade until the 18th century – and the loss of Barcelona's prerogatives after its conquest in 1714 by the troops of Philip V, who made the Catalans pay with their blood for any aspirations to independence, marked the city's decline. It went on to experience a new period of growth in the 19th century, with the simultaneous appearance of the cultural movement known as the Renaixença – which breathed new life into Catalan culture and its language – and of industrialization, which brought to the fore the entrepreneurial talents of Barcelona's citizens. The 1888 Universal Exhibition and the 1929 International Exhibition allowed the city, which had remained within its original walls until the mid-19th century, to expand and enrich itself with new monuments ➡88, 90, 98. So an important city planning scheme, known as the Eixample, was dreamed up by Ildefons Cerdà. This ambitious project was threatened by the greed of property speculators and was only partially realized: thus, although it was planned that only two sides of each city block would be bounded by buildings, all four sides were built up; a great many houses designed by renowned architects were knocked down to make way for characterless buildings. Nevertheless, Barcelona is undoubtedly the European city in which the Modernist style – known elsewhere as Art Nouveau or Jugendstil – achieved its most eloquent architectural expression ➡94, 98. The historical vicissitudes of the 19th century have left a deep mark on the spirit of Barcelona's

i Ocell', a sculpture by Miró (6); the Palau Sant Jordi, built for the 1992 Olympic Games (7).

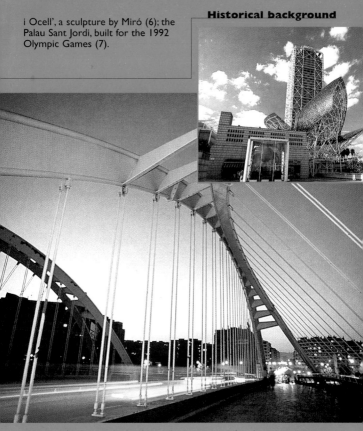

citizens, who have ceaselessly sought recognition for their autonomy – a recognition which the dictatorships of Primo de Rivera (1923–31) and Franco (1939–76) always stubbornly and brutally denied. In the first half of the 20th century Barcelona was the center of the anarchist movement: in May 1937, even though democratic Spain's desperate armed resistance against Franco's troops had already begun, the anarchists and the Communists were fighting each other in Barcelona. After the restoration of democracy, following a referendum in December 1976, the autonomous institutions were reconstituted, having ceased to exist since the period of the Republic (1936–9). The city rapidly wiped over the traces of forty years of dictatorship, and for the last twenty years it has lived through another golden age, which has been intensified by its nomination as the host of the Olympic Games in 1992. The city is now equipped with state-of-the-art sporting facilities ➡96, and it has taken advantage of the Games to redefine its city planning, and turn Barcelona once again toward the sea, which for centuries had been little more than a natural backdrop ➡90. The Olympic Games have contributed to the promotion of Barcelona, and since 1992 the number of foreign visitors has increased considerably. Aware of the impact that the organization of high profile events can have on both the city's image and the rehabilitation of rundown neighborhoods, the Catalan authorities have decided to launch the Barcelona 2004 project, with a wide-ranging program which aims to turn Barcelona into one of the world's centers for cultural activities.

In the area

The historic heart of the city, the Barri Gòtic, with its maze of alleyways and its delightful little squares, has retained its medieval charm, which reflects the power of Catalonia in the Mediterranean basin at that time. However, it also bears important traces of a more recent past.

What to see

Catedral (1)

Pla de la Seu - 08002 ☎ 93 315 15 54 / 93 315 22 13

Ⓜ *Jaume I* 🕐 *Sun.–Fri. 8am–1.30pm, 4–7.30pm; Sat. 9am–1pm, 5–7pm* ● *free* ♿ *Chancel* 🕐 *Mon.–Sat. 10am–12.30pm, 4–6.30pm* ● *125 Ptas* *Cloister* 🕐 *9am–1pm, 4–7pm* ● *free* **Museum** 🕐 *Mon.–Sat. 10am–1pm, 4–7pm; Sun. 10am–1pm* ● *100 Ptas* **Elevator** 🕐 *Mon.–Fri. 10.30am–1pm, 4.30–6pm; Sat. 10.30am–1pm* ● *200 Ptas*

Building work on the Gothic cathedral, an imposing monument comprising three vaulted naves and a single apse, began in 1298, but the façade and the spire, 230 ft high, were not finished until the turn of the 20th century. Consecrated to Saint Eulalia, the patron saint of Barcelona, the cathedral houses many treasures, such as the chancel adorned with a sculpted marble screen and finely carved stalls from the 15th century; the alabaster sarcophagus of Saint Eulalia on display in the crypt and the much venerated Christ of Lepanto (in the chapel of the Holy Sacrament, on the right, at the entrance to the cathedral). The impressive cloister, bounded by arches and planted with palm trees and magnolias, is connected to the 12th-century chapel of Saint Lucia and, via an elevator, to the terraces on the cathedral roof, which afford a dizzying view of the city.

Plaça del Rei (2)

Ⓜ *Jaume I*

This is one of the most picturesque squares in the whole of Barcelona. It is the site of the Palau del Lloctinent, to the rear, and the impressive watch tower of King Martí, both dating from the 15th century, as well as the more heterogeneous buildings of the Palau Reial Major, with Roman foundations but a Gothic appearance. It also houses the Gothic portal of the Palatine chapel (or Saint Agueda's chapel) and the Padellàs building, in a Catalan Gothic style, the home of the museum of the city's history.

Palau de la Música Catalana (3)

Carrer Sant Pere Més Alt, 4 - 08003 ☎ 93 268 10 00

Ⓜ *Jaume I* 🕐 *Nov.–May. Tue., Thu. 2pm, 3pm; Sat., 11am, noon, 1pm; June–Oct. on request* ● *1,500 Ptas* 📷

A Modernist masterpiece, the Palau de la Música was built between 1905 and 1908 by Domènech i Montaner. The decoration on the façade, consisting entirely of colored mosaics, echoes the imposing inverted polychrome glass cupola of the concert hall.

Not forgetting

■ **Plaça Sant Felip Neri (4)** *A charming little square, with a 19th-century palace and fountain.* ■ **Plaça Sant Jaume (5)** *This square, the center of the city's political life, houses the Palau de la Generalitat, the seat of Catalonia's autonomous government, and Barcelona's Ajuntament (City Hall), with the unmissable Gothic Hall of the Consell de Cent..* ■ **Museu d'Història de la Ciutat (6)** *Carrer Veguer, 4 - 08002 ☎ 93 315 11 11* 🕐 *Tue.–Sat. 10am–2pm, 4–8pm Interesting collection of works of art and documents on Barcelona. The palace leads to the Palatine chapel and the underground galleries, which display the remains of the Roman city.* ■ **Casa de l'Ardiaca (7)** *Carrer Santa Llúcia, 1 - 08002 ☎ 93 318 11 95 This 15th-century house has a delightful patio.*

The Palau de la Música Catalana, a modernist jewel in the heart of the medieval part of the city.

In the area

The Ribera neighborhood was a particular beneficiary of the Catalans' maritime and commercial expansion in the Mediterranean, although it fell into decline in 1714 when Philip V brutally repressed any aspirations to Catalan independence. Today, fine old buildings house major museums.

What to see

Carrer Montcada (8-11)

Museu Tèxtil Carrer Montcada, 12 - 08003 ☎ 93 310 45 16 🅼 Arc de Triomf 🚇 17, 19, 40, 45 🕐 Tue.–Sat. 10am–8pm, Sundays and public holidays 10am–3pm ● 1,500 Ptas; first Saturday of the month free 3–8pm 🔲 🖥 ♿ ⊞
Museu Barbier-Mueller Carrer Montcada, 14 - 08003 ☎ 93 319 76 03 🅼 Arc de Triomf 🚇 17, 19, 40, 45 🕐 Tue.–Sat. 10am–8pm, Sundays and public holidays 10am–3pm ● 1,500 Ptas; first Saturday of the month free 3–8pm 🔲 🖥 ♿ ⊞
Museu Picasso Carrer Montcada, 15–19, 08003 ☎ 93 319 63 10 🅼 Arc de Triomf 🚇 17, 19, 40, 45 🕐 Tue.–Sat., public holidays 10am–8pm; Sun. 10am–3pm ● 700 Ptas; first Sunday of the month free 🔲 🍴 ♿ ⊞
Galeria Maeght Carrer Montcada, 25 - 08003 ☎ 93 310 42 45 🅼 Arc de Triomf 🚇 17, 19, 40, 45 🕐 Tue.–Sat. 10am–2pm, 4pm–8pm ● free

The main mansions on this thoroughfare, home to the area's powerful merchants from the 13th to the 17th centuries, are today the setting for the city's great museums. The 12th-century palace of the Marquess of Liló, built around a charming patio, which is now the crowning glory of a small bar, houses the extensive fabric collection of the **Museu Tèxtil y de Indumentària (8)**, which traces six centuries of the history of textiles. Next door, the **Museu Barbier-Mueller (9)** displays pre-Colombian art. Across the street, the palace of the Baron de Castellet i Meca joins forces with the Berenguer d'Aguilar Palace to accommodate the **Museu Picasso (10)**, which exhibits the master's early works. Particularly outstanding are the Meninas series, variations on the Velázquez painting, and the Sabartés collection of Picasso's graphic work. The 15th-century Cervelló Palace houses the **Galerie Maeght (11)**, a leading light in the field of modern and contemporary art.

Basílica de Santa Maria del Mar (12)
Plaça Santa Maria, 1 - 08003 ☎ 93 310 23 90

🅼 Arc de Triomf 🕐 daily 9am–1pm, 4.30–8pm ♿

Work on the sanctuary, financed by the neighborhood's merchants and ship-owners, began after the glorious expedition undertaken by King Alfons in 1329, which secured Sardinia for Catalonia. The intensity of the construction period not only allowed this basilica to be completed by 1384, but also meant that it can claim an extraordinary stylistic harmony. Even though the interior has had to be restored twice, after fires in 1714 and 1939, it is still the most authentic example of Catalan Gothic in Barcelona, and the perfect proportions and grandeur of its interior are awe-inspiring. This church, designed for preaching, is dominated by horizontal lines, wide spaces, large bare surfaces, massive buttresses and tiered roofs.

Not forgetting

■ **Mercat del Born (13)** Carrer del Comerç *This huge building, a beautiful example of metallic architecture put up by the engineer Josep M. Carnet i Mas in 1876, represented a partial return to the neighborhood's former role as a trading center. In fact, it was Barcelona's main market until 1971. It will soon be the home of the provincial library.* ■ **Arc de Triomf (14)** Passeig Lluís Companys *Built in 1888 as a monumental gateway to the Universal Exhibition, this 140-ft brick-built arch is evidence of the neo-Mudejar style which was fashionable in this period.*

In the area

This park, much loved by the locals, occupies the site of the military fortress built by Philip V after the defeat of Barcelona in 1714. This symbol of the repression of the city's civil liberties was destroyed during the resurgence of Catalan nationalism in the second half of the 19th

What to see

Parc de la Ciutadella (15-20)

Ⓜ *Ciutadella* 🕐 *Apr.–Sep. 8am–9pm; Oct.–May 8am–8pm* **Parc Zoològic** ☎ *93 225 67 80* 🕐 *10am–6pm* ● *1,400 Ptas; under-12s, 950 Ptas; over-65s, 800 Ptas* **Museu d'Art Modern** ☎ *93 319 50 23* 🕐 *Tue.–Sat. 10am–7pm; Sundays and public holidays 10am–2.30pm* ● *500 Ptas; first Thursday of the month free* 🔲 🔲 ♿ **Museu de Geología** ☎ *93 319 68 95* 🕐 *Tue.–Sun., public holidays 10am–2pm; Thu. 10am–6.30pm* ● *400 Ptas; free for under-12s, and on the first Sunday of the month*

The park was created in 1871 when the municipality accepted the plan drawn up by Josep Fontserè i Mestres, which sought to turn the old military fort into the city's green lung. The fruits of this first phase of construction can still be seen in the gates, lamp posts, fountain, conservatories and wrought iron work. In 1888 it housed the Universal Exhibition, and in 1892 one third of the surface area was given over to the **Parc Zoològic (15)**. The construction of the waterfall **Cascada (16)** began in 1874, following a plan by Fontserè which also drew on the participation of the young Antoni Gaudí. This Modernist monument was unveiled in 1881, although it was not finished until 1888. It is crowned by a quadriga, decorated with a statue of Aurora. **The Hivernacle (17)**, a greenhouse designed by Josep Armagós Samaranch and built between 1883 and 1887, is a beautiful example of late 19th-century architecture in iron and glass. Its large glass canopy now presides over a pleasant café. **The Umbracle (18)**, an enormous conservatory designed to protect shade-loving plants, offers a remarkable play of light and shade on sunny days. The center of the park is taken up by an 18th-century building which was once the citadel's arsenal, before being used as the royal residence. It now houses the **Museu d'Art Modern (19)** and, in its inner chambers, the parliament for the autonomous community of Catalonia. The museum's exhibits include paintings typical of Catalan Modernism and Neo-Impressionism, along with sculptures by Josep Clarà and Modernist furniture. The park also contains the **Museu de Geología (20)**, the oldest museum in Barcelona, which first opened in 1887.

Port Olímpic (21)

Ⓜ *Ciutadella*

The Olympic port, in the Poble Nou neighborhood, is now completely given over to sport and leisure activities. Its refurbishment reflects the vision of architects like Bohigas, Martorell, Mackay and Puigdomènech, which was brought to life by the engineer Joan Ramon Clascà. The locals, equally drawn by the nearby Nova Icària beach, love to pass their time in the port's countless shops, bars and restaurants, which are open seven days a week ...

Not forgetting

■ **Vila Olímpica (22)** *Built to accommodate the athletes participating in the 1992 Olympics, the village replaced an old working-class neighborhood. Its 2,000 apartments, surrounded by greenery and designed by top Catalan architects, enjoy an unbeatable view of the sea. The Olympic Village has become a very popular residential area.* ■ **Escultura del Peix (23)** *Carrer Marina The work of Frank Gehry, the creator of the Bilbao Guggenheim, this golden whale, seemingly beached outside the Arts Hotel, is one of the symbol's of contemporary Barcelona.*

century and turned into a park, before serving as the site for the Universal Exhibition in 1888.

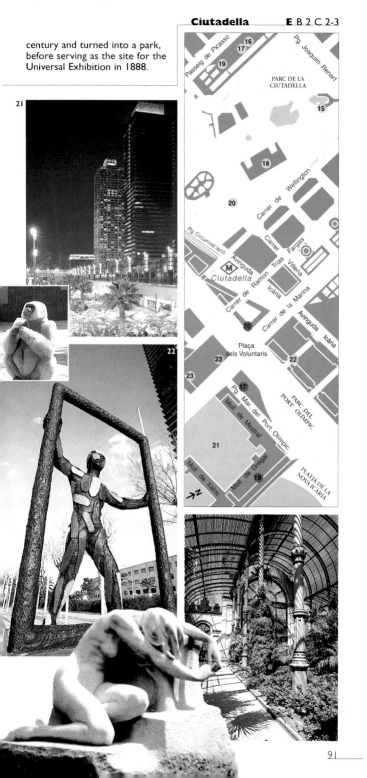

In the area

The Rambla, which connects Plaça Catalunya with the monument to Christopher Columbus, overlooking the sea, is Barcelona's most lively and colorful thoroughfare. Its lifeblood flows through it both night and day, among the sellers of flowers and birds, the café terraces and the

What to see

Monumento a Colón (24)
Plaça Portal de la Pau, 1 - 08002

◼ Drassanes. ◯ Mon.–Fri. 10am–1.30pm, 3.30–6.30pm; Sat., Sun. and public holidays 10am–6.30pm ● 250 Ptas ◼

Situated at the bottom of the Rambla, facing the sea, the monument to Christopher Columbus, erected by Gaietà Buigas Monravà in 1880, commemorates the reception given in honor of the Genoan navigator on his return from the New World by King Ferdinand and Queen Isabel. Perched atop a cast-iron column, the explorer does not point toward America but to the Mediterranean, the source of Barcelona's wealth.

Plaça Reial (25)

◼ Liceu

Linked to the Rambla by the Calle Colom and the striking Passeig Bacardi, an iron and glass gallery inspired by its Parisian counterparts, this square was built between 1858 and 1860, on the basis of plans drawn up by Francesc Daniel Molina. It is a charming place to have lunch or a drink, underneath the arches or in the shade of a palm tree. Gaudí designed the street-lamps and the fountain of the Three Graces.

MACBA (26)
Plaça dels Àngels, 1 - 08001 ☎ 93 412 08 10

◼ Catalunya ◯ Mon., Wed., Fri. noon–8pm; Thu. 10am–9.30pm; Sat. 10am–8pm; Sun. and public holidays 10am–3pm ● 700 Ptas; Wed. 375 Ptas ◻ ◼ ☎ 934121413 ⊞ ▮ ⊞ ◼ **CCCB** Carrer Montalegre, 5 08001 ☎ 93 306 41 00 ◼ Catalunya ◯ Tue., Fri. 11am–2pm, 4pm–8pm; Wed., Sat. 11am–8pm; Thu. 11am–2pm, 4pm–9.30pm; Sun. and public holidays 11am–7pm ● 600 Ptas; Wed. 400 Ptas

Barcelona's Contemporary Art Museum, in the heart of the working-class Raval district, was opened in November 1995. It plays host to the latest trends in international and Catalan art. The building, designed by the American architect Richard Meier, is made up of three floors bathed in natural light, and its white mass contrasts with the murky side-streets of the run-down neighborhood, which is in the process of being renovated. Next to the MACBA there is a beautiful palace, complete with a delightful patio, which houses the CCCB, an arts center which puts on exhibitions and multi-disciplinary events.

Not forgetting

◼ **Drassanes (27)** Avinguda de les Drassanes - 08001 ☎ 93 301 18 31 ◯ Tue.–Sun. 10am–7pm ● 800 Ptas *Situated at the bottom of the Rambla, near the Columbus monument, the former royal arsenal is now home to the Maritime Museum. The highlight is the life-size copy of the REAL, the famous flagship of Don Juan of Austria, the commander of the Christian fleet at the battle of Lepant (1571).* ◼ **Casa Bruno Quadros (28)** Pla de la Boquería - 08002 *This Japanese-style house was designed by Josep Vilaseca in 1883. Outside, the Rambla has a mosaic of paving stones created by Miró in the 1970s.* ◼ **Santa Maria del Pi (29)** Plaça del Pi - 08002 ☎ 93 318 47 43 ◯ 8.30am–1pm, 4.30–9pm *Church with a single nave, a polygonal apse and an impressive rose-window. A beautiful example of Gatalan Gothic.*

street artists – actors, musicians
or living statues.

26

29

25

28

24

Map labels:

Catalunya

26
C. Tallers
Pl. Vicenç Martorell   72 37 31
Pl. Angels   34 6
C. dels Angels   Pl. Bonsucces
Carrer del Pintor Fortuny   7
Rbla. Estudis
Rbla. Canaletes
C. Canuda
36 Pl. Vila de Madrid
8
9
Carrer   del   Carme   32
31
Pl. de la Gardunya   43
C. Portaferrissa
C. Josep
Sant
Carrer d'en Roca
29
Carrer   Hospital   26 30 25   28
1   29
C. S.Rafael   28   Pl. Sant Agustí   Rbla.
Liceu   C. Boqueria
M   14 27
C. d'en Robidor
Junta de Comerç   12   Pau   10 1
Caputxins
24 45
Carrer de Sant   Carrer Unió   11
10 25 26
C. Marq. de Barbera   Rambla   Rbla.
Carrer Nou de la Rambla
27
Carrer   Avinguda   del   C. Guardia   Teatre   9
C. Montserrat
Rbla. Sta. Monica
Carrer Arc del
Carrer Cid
de les   Drassanes
Portal de S. Madrona   M   28 23
Drassanes
Pl. Portal de la Pau
Av. del Paral·lel   Carrer
27
C. de S. Carrera
24

N

The figurehead of Modernism, Antoni Gaudi (1852–1926), created a visionary body of work in Barcelona, with dynamic forms which caused great controversy in their time but later earned him recognition as one of the greatest architects of all time. Examples of his work can be seen

What to see

Sagrada Família (30)
Carrer Mallorca, 401 - 08013 ☎ 93 455 02 47

Ⓜ *Sagrada Familia* 🕐 *9am–7pm* ● *800 Ptas; free for under-10s* ♿ ⊞

The Sagrada Família is undoubtedly the symbol of the city and Gaudí's most famous monument. In 1891 the architect, commissioned to build a neo-Gothic church, transformed the initial project to create an audacious work imbued with religious symbolism, which would occupy him to his death in 1926. Although the master could not complete his project – of the three enormous facades, he only lived to see one, that of the Nativity – work was restarted, not without fierce controversy, by his students and it is still continuing today … The façade of the Passion was put up in 1986 by the sculptor Josep Maria Subirachs. In the crypt, where Gaudí was buried, there is an exhibition of plans, models, drawings and photographs.

Parc Güell (31)
Carretera del Carmel - 08024 ☎ 93 424 38 09

▦ *24, 25* 🕐 *May–Aug. 10am–9pm; Nov.-Feb. 10am–6pm; Mar., Oct. 10am–7pm; Apr., Sep. 10am–8pm* ● *free* ▣ *Gaudí's house* ☎ 93 219 38 11 🕐 *May–Sep. 10am–8pm; Nov.-Feb. 10am–6pm; Mar.–Apr., Oct. 10am–7pm*
● *300 pesetas*

The most famous of the commissions made to Gaudí by Eusebi Güell was intended to be a utopian city-garden, but this ambitious project was never brought to fruition through lack of funds, and only two houses were ever built. The park's most impressive features include the staircase, dominated by a mosaic dragon and a fountain, the Hundred Pillar hall (designed to be the market-place) and the long undulating bench, decorated by Josep M. Jujol, a close collaborator of Gaudí. It is

throughout the city in large
and small projects.

With its soaring
spires, the Sagrada
Família has become
the undisputed
symbol of Barcelona.

also possible to visit the project's show-
house, where Gaudí himself lived for twenty
years, from 1906 to 1926.

Casa Milà-La Pedrera (32)
Passeig de Gràcia, 92 - 08007
☎ 93 484 59 95

M Diagonal, Passeig de Gràcia. *Gallery* 🕐 daily
10am–8pm ● free. *Espai Gaudí* 🕐 daily
10am–8pm (until midnight in summer) ● 500 Ptas
🍴 Ⓨ 🖵 ⊞

The sinuous lines of the façade, decorated with
wrought-iron balconies, reflect the disturbing
forms of the chimneys on the roof, which
evoke knights in armor. La Pedrera (1905–10)
houses the Espai Gaudí, a small museum
devoted to the architect.

Not forgetting

■ **Casa Batlló (33)** Passeig de Gràcia, 43 -
08007 Not open to visitors. The undulating façade,
in the heart of the 'Block of Discord' ➡ 100, is
topped off with strange balconies in the form of
masks. The decoration, in ceramics and glass, was the work of Jujol. ■ **Palau
Güell (34)** Carrer Nou de la Rambla, 3 - 08001 ☎ 93 317 39 74
🕐 Mon.– Fri. 10.15am, 10.45am, 11.30am, noon, 12.30pm, 1pm, 4pm,
4.30pm, 5pm, 5.30pm, 6pm, 6.30pm ● 400 Ptas 🎫 This palace (1885–9) is
distinguished by the parabolic arches in the entrance, which are rounded off by sinuous
grilles, and the fantastic chimneys on the roof, which anticipated those of the Pedrera.

In the area

The southern slope of the Montjuïc hill was chosen as the site for the sports complex used in the 1992 Olympics. The modernity of these installations provides a striking contrast with the citadel, the site of the infamous military prison during the dictatorships, now a museum.

What to see

Anella Olímpica (35-38)
Parc de Montjuïc - 08038

🖼 *50 Olympic stadium. Palau Sant Jordi* ◐ *daily 10am–6pm* ● *free Picornell swimming pools* ☎ *93 423 40 41* ◐ *summer: Mon.–Sat. 9am–8pm; Sun. and public holidays 9am–8pm* ● *650 Ptas winter: Mon.–Sat. 7am–midnight; Sun. and public holidays 7.30am–2.30pm* ● *1,200 Ptas; 650 Ptas for under-12s*

The **stadium (35)**, built on the site of the old Montjuïc stadium, preserves part of the old structure. When the first stadium was opened in 1929 it was the second largest stadium in Europe, only surpassed by Wembley in London. The new stadium, the result of a collaboration between the architects Correa, Milà, Margarit, Buixadé and Gregotti, holds 55,000 people, and was the stage for the opening and closing ceremonies of the 1992 Olympics; it is now the setting for the home games of the RCD Espanyol soccer club, concerts and some of the city's special occasions. The sculpture by Paul Gargallo 'Two Knights Giving the Olympic Salute' dominates the Marathon Entrance, while the same artist's 'Auriga' has pride of place on the main façade. Nearby, there is the soaring **Palau Sant Jordi (36),** with its spectacular 80-ton cupola, 470 ft high. This pavilion, in the form of an enormous sleeping tortoise, designed by the Japanese architect Arata Isozaki, astonished local residents, and many of them consider it a symbol of the modernity of this new Montjuïc district. Used for concerts and sporting events, it has a capacity of 17,000 people. Outside, the forest of street-lamps, veritable light sculptures, is the work of Isozaki's wife, Aiko Mijawaki. The complex also contains the **Bernat Picornell swimming pools (37),** built for the 1970 European swimming championships and refurbished for the 1992 Olympics. They lie in the shadow of the **Torre Calatrava (38)**, a tall telecommunications tower named after its creator, the engineer Santiago Calatrava. This daringly designed antenna also serves as a meridian, as its form corresponds to the angle of the summer solstice in Barcelona.

Castell de Montjuïc (39)
Parque de Montjuïc - 08038 ☎ 93 329 86 13

🖼 *61 + telefèric del Montjuic* ◐ *Tue.–Sun. 10am–8pm* ● *200 Ptas* ▣ ▨

This fortress was put up in a mere thirty days in 1640, when Barcelona's citizens rebelled against the Castilian monarchy and placed themselves under the protection of the French. However, the revolt failed, and the castle, perched on the top of the hill, overlooking the city, became a symbol of repression, as it was the headquarters for the crushing of all popular uprisings for centuries. Under the dictatorship of Franco, thousands of political prisoners were imprisoned there, and many important Catalan figures, such as the educationalist Francesc Ferrer i Guàrdia and Lluís Companys, the President of the Generalitat in the years of the Republic, were executed there. It has now been given over to the city and houses the Museu Militar, which has a valuable collection of ancient weapons. The ramparts provide a breathtaking panoramic view of Barcelona.

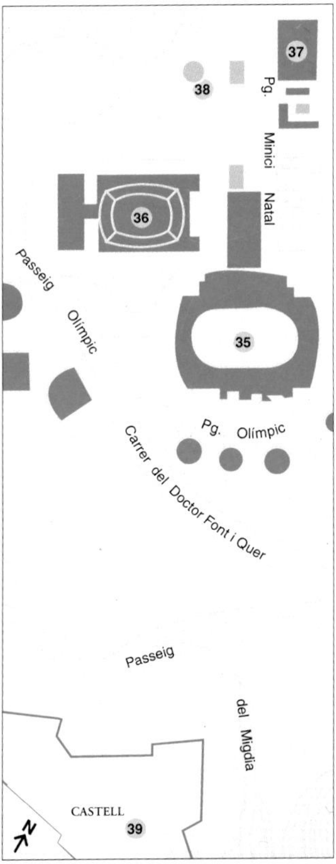
37
38
Pg.
Minici
Natal
36
Passeig
Olímpic
35
Pg.
Olímpic
Carrer del Doctor Font i Quer
Passeig
del
Migdia
CASTELL
39
N

In the area

In 1929 the Montjuïc hill was chosen as the site of the International Exhibition: major buildings were put up and elegant gardens were created on the hill's flanks. Coming from the Plaça Espanya, it is reached by passing through the colonnade and following the Avinguda Reina Maria Cristina.

What to see

Palau Nacional/MNAC (40)
Parc de Montjuïc - 08038 ☎ 93 423 71 99 ➡ 93 325 57 73

▣ 61 ◑ Tue.–Sat. 10am–7pm; Thu. 10am–9pm; Sun. and public holidays 10am–2.30pm ● 800 Ptas ▣ ▣ ▦

This was the centerpiece of the 1929 International Exhibition. Designed by the architects Eugeni P. Cendoya and Enric Català i Català in 1924, during the dictatorship of General Primo de Rivera, this monumental palace, eclectic in style, affords a remarkable vista of the Avinguda Reina Maria Cristina and the Plaça Espanya. It was refurbished in 1990 by the Italian Gae Aulenti, the architect of the Orsay Museum in Paris, to house the Museu Nacional d'Art de Catalunya (MNAC). Since 1995, the Romanesque art section presents, highly informatively, the largest collection of medieval frescos in Europe, taken from small churches in the Pyrenees, while the Gothic art section, opened in 1997, presents a superb selection of altarpieces.

Pavelló Mies van der Rohe (41)
Avda. Marquès de Comillas - 08038 ☎ 93 423 40 16 ➡ 93 426 37 72

▣ 61 ◑ Apr.–Oct. 10am–8pm; Nov.–Mar. 10am–6.30pm ● 300 Ptas; free for under-18s ♿

The building of the pavilion representing Germany in the 1929 Exhibition was entrusted to Ludwig Mies van der Rohe. Like all the pavilions, it was subsequently demolished when the event finished, but this building, which the dean of Barcelona's architecture school considered 'an obligatory reference in 20th-century art and architecture', was nevertheless reconstructed, down to the last detail, in 1986, in anticipation of the Olympic Games. Inside, documentation on the architect can be seen.

Font Màgica (42)
Avinguda Reina Maria Cristina

▣ Fri.–Sun. and public holidays, displays every half-hour (7–9pm)

Also built for the 1929 Exhibition, this huge fountain, with jets of water which change form and color in time with music, stunned the crowds when it was unveiled. It was restored in 1954–5 by its creator, the engineer Carles Buïgas. A truly magical spot, it enhances the impact of the concerts and firework displays which take place nearby.

Not forgetting

■ **Poble Espanyol (43)** Avinguda Marquès de Comillas - 08038 ☎ 93 325 78 66 ◑ Mon. 9am–8pm; Tue.–Thu. 9am–2am; Fri., Sat. and the days before public holidays 9am–4am; Sun. and public holidays 9am–midnight ▣ ▦ ▼ ▦ *A legacy of the 1929 Exhibition, this village offers a resumé, in each of its streets and squares, of the architecture of the different regions in Spain. Folkloric festivals and fairs all help to liven the place up even more.* ■ **Fundació Miró (44)** Avinguda Miramar, 71 - 08038 ☎ 93 329 19 08 ◑ Tue.–Sat. 10am–7pm; Thu. 10am–9.30pm; Sunday and public holidays 10am–2.30pm ● 800 Ptas ▣ ▦ ▦ *The dreamchild of Joan Miró (1893–1983), this cultural center, endowed with some 10,000 works by the Catalan artist, also puts on exhibitions of 20th-century art.*

43

42

40

99

Gaudí was not the only Modernist architect to be acclaimed in Barcelona. Lluís Domènech i Montaner (1850–1923) and Josep Puig i Cadalfalch (1867–1957) are also worthy representatives of this highly innovative artistic trend. Most of their buildings are concentrated in the neighborhood of the Eixample, the extension to the city drawn up in the

What to see

Manzana de la Discordia (46-47)
Passeig de Gràcia, 35/43 - 08007

Ⓜ *Passeig de Gràcia*

This cluster of buildings on the Passeig de Gràcia, between Carrer Consell de Cent and Carrer Aragó, owes its nickname ('block of discord') to the different architectural styles of the three Modernist masters, each responsible for one building here: the floral motifs of Domènech i Montaner for the Casa Lleó Morera **(46)**, at number 35; the extravagant gables and ceramic decorations of Puig i Cadafalch for the Casa Amatller **(47)**, at number 41, and the undulating fairytale forms of the balconies and roof dreamed up by Gaudí for the Casa Batlló, at number 43 ➡ 94.

Hospital de la Santa Creu i Sant Pau (48)
Carrer Sant Antoni Maria Claret, 167/171 - 08025 ☎ 93 291 90 00

Ⓜ *Sant Pau*

This hospital complex, designed by Domènech i Montaner in 1901, is made up of a series of independent pavilions, surrounded by gardens and interconnected by a network of underground passageways, and covers nine blocks in the Eixample neighborhood. In 1914 the architect's son, Pere Domènech i Roura, took charge of the project and introduced some new baroque elements, and by 1930 the hospital was fully functioning.

45

46

47

50

19th century.

Casa Macaya/Centre Cultural de la Fundació 'la Caixa' (49)
Passeig de Sant Joan, 108 - 08037 ☎ 93 458 89 07 / 93 458 13 08

M *Verdaguer* ◯ *Tue.–Sat. 11am–8pm; Sun. and public holidays 11am–3pm* ●
300 Ptas; Sat. free ▯ ▯ ♿ ▦

This small palace, built in 1901, is the work of Puig i Cadafalch. Its brilliant white façade is flanked by two lateral towers topped off by a roof with four slopes. It houses a major cultural center and a multimedia library.

Fundació Tàpies (50)
Carrer Aragó, 255 - 08007 ☎ 93 487 03 15 / 93 487 00 09

M *Passeig de Gràcia* ◯ *Tue.–Sun. 11am–8pm* ● *500 Ptas* ▯ ♿ ▦

One of the earliest Modernist buildings, this building (1880) is now the headquarters of the Fundació Tàpies, set up to promote contemporary art and exhibit the works of the Barcelona painter Antoni Tàpies, born in 1923. The artist has also contributed the metal wire sculpture on top of the building, 'Clouds and Chair'.

Not forgetting

■ **Palau del Baró de Quadras/Museu de la Música (51)** Avinguda Diagonal, 373 - 08013 ☎ 93 416 11 57 **M** Diagonal ◯ Tue.–Sun. 10am–2pm; Wed. 10am–8pm ● 400 Ptas *The work of Puig i Cadafalch, this palace (1904-1906) houses the music museum. The architect refurbished an existing building and incorporated Gothic elements and sculptures by Eusebi Arnau into the façade.*

In the area

For the residents of Barcelona, Pedralbes is the epitome of a chic neighborhood. Elegant residences are complemented by historical buildings or ones with symbolic value for the Catalan identity, such as Camp Nou, the home of the legendary Barcelona Football Club.

What to see

Monestir de Pedralbes (52)
Baixada Monestir, 9 - 08034 ☎ 93 203 92 82 / 93 203 94 08

Ⓜ *Palau Reial* ▣ *22, 63, 64, 75, 78* Ⓒ *Tue.–Sun. 10am–2pm* ● *400 Ptas; first Sun. of the month free* ♿ **Collecció Thyssen-Bornemisza** Ⓒ *Tue.–Sun. 10am–2pm* ● *400 Ptas* ▤ ♿ ⊞

Founded in 1326 by Elisenda de Montcada, the Queen of Aragon and the fourth wife of Jaume II, the monastery was designed by Ferrer Peiró, who built it in conjunction with Domènec Granyer. A perfectly preserved masterpiece of Catalan Gothic architecture, it has been inhabited for centuries by a closed order of nuns, the Clares. However, it is possible to visit the capitular hall, abbey, refectory, cloister, kitchen and communal areas. The triple gallery of arches in the Gothic-style cloister – the largest in Europe – provide the setting for a garden with orange trees and palms. Frescos dating from the 14th century, the period of the original construction, have been discovered in one of the chapels. The 72 paintings from the Thyssen-Bornemisza collection, on display here since 1993, offer an interesting overview of the European schools.

Estadi del FC Barcelona (Camp Nou) (53)
Carrer Arístides Maillol, 12-18 - 08028 ☎ 93 496 36 08 / 93 411 22 19

Ⓜ *Palau Reial* **Barça Museum** Ⓒ *Mon.–Sat. 10am–6.30pm; Sun. and public holidays 10am–2pm* ● *475 Ptas; free for members of Barcelona FC* ⊞

Fervent soccer fans know that Barça (the affectionate abbreviation of a club which has long been the main symbol of Catalan identity) is 'more than a club': it is an institution ... All its games – and victories – unleash passions! The stadium, one of the biggest in Europe, was built in 1957 after a design by Francesc Mitjans. This huge concrete arena, covering 300,000 sq. ft, has a capacity of some 109,000 spectators. Devotees can also visit the Barça Museum, which chronicles the history of the club since its foundation in 1889.

Palau Reial de Pedralbes (54)
Avinguda Diagonal, 686 - 08034 ☎ 93 280 13 64

Garden Ⓒ *from 10am to sunset* **Museu de les Arts Decoratives** ☎ *93 280 50 24* Ⓒ *Sun. and public holidays 10am–3pm* ● *400 Ptas; 250 Ptas for students; first Sunday of the month free* **Museu de Ceràmica** ☎ *93 280 16 21* Ⓒ *Tue.–Sat. 10am–6pm; Sun. and public holidays 10am–3pm* ● *400 Ptas; 250 Ptas for students; the first Sunday of the month free*

The royal palace of Pedralbes, inspired by Italian Renaissance mansions, was finished in 1929 thanks to a popular subscription organized by the Catalan aristocracy, who wanted King Alfonso XIII to have a residence in Barcelona ... The royal family had in effect deserted the Catalan capital in 1875, after the fire in their former palace (on the site of the present-day Plaça del Palau). The surrounding garden is extremely beautiful. An annex to the palace houses the Museum of Decorative Arts, which affords a historical tour of the applied arts and also provides a glimpse of the more recent trends in Catalonia. For its part, the Ceramics Museum traces the evolution of the decorations, forms and clays used in Spanish pottery from the 12th century to the present.

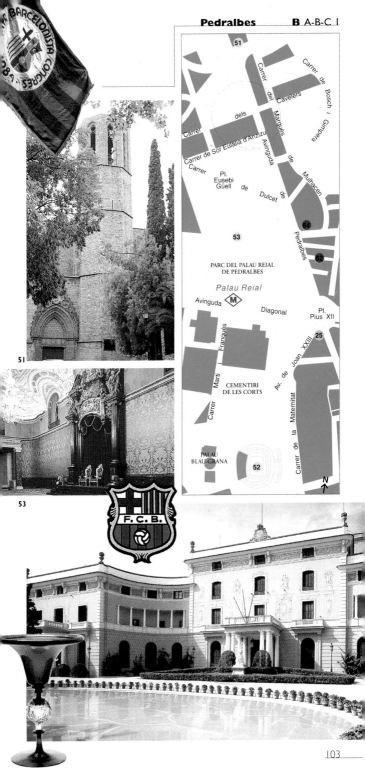

51

53

PARC DEL PALAU REIAL
DE PEDRALBES

Palau Reial

CEMENTIRI
DE LES CORTS

PALAU
BLAU-GRANA

In the area

Tibidabo undoubtedly offers the most spectacular views of Barcelona: its peak (1,600 ft) towers over the checkerboard of the Eixample, and on a clear day one can see the Pyrenees. These days the hill is entirely given over to the pursuit of pleasure ...

What to see

Parc de Atraccions del Tibidabo (55)
Plaça del Tibidabo - 08035 ☎ 93 221 79 42

🚠 *funicular de Vallvidrera + bus 211; school holidays: tranvia blau + funicular de Tibidabo* 🕓 *Mar.–Oct.: Wed.–Fri. 10am–6pm; Sat., Sun. and public holidays noon–9pm* ● *2,400 Ptas; 600 Ptas for children, the disabled and over 60s* 🏪
🍽 🚻 *Museu d'Autòmats* 🕓 *Mar.–Oct.: Wed.–Fri. 10am–6pm; Sat., Sun. and public holidays noon–9pm* ● ● *2,400 Ptas; 600 Ptas for children, the disabled and over 60s*

The Tibidabo fairground has been operating intermittently ever since 1905: some rides, such as the aerial train (1915), the star turn (1921) and the airplane (1928) gave it an old-fashioned charm, in contrast with the more recent installations, which include the terrifying Krüeger Hotel. The Museu d'Autòmats, with one of the biggest collections of automatons and mechanical toys in Europe, will delight young and old.

Temple del Sagrat Cor (56)
Plaça del Tibidabo - 08035 ☎ 93 417 56 86 / 93 434 01 90

🚠 *funicular de Vallvidrera + bus 211; school holidays: tranvia blau + funicular de Tibidabo* 🕓 *daily 10am–7pm Elevator Mon. 11am–2pm; 3pm–7pm; Tue.–Fri. 10am–2pm, 3pm–7pm; Sat. and public holidays 10am–2pm; 4pm–8pm* ● *100 Ptas*

The origins of this Temple to the Sacred Heart of Jesus lie in a small sanctuary built in 1886 in order to celebrate the visit of Dom Bosco to Barcelona. The construction of the present-day church began in 1902, based on a design by Enric Sagnier (1858–1931). This building, with its eclectic mix of styles, completed in 1961 with the placing of an image of the Sacred Heart on its pinnacle, is undoubtedly the most controversial of the works of this prolific architect. The sanctuary, lit up at night, is visible from all parts of the city. Its terrace, which can be reached by elevator, offers a breathtaking 180° panoramic view which, on clear days, embraces Montserrat ➡ 110 and the Pyrenees.

Torre de Collserola (57)
Carr. de Vallvidrera al Tibidabo - 08035 ☎ 93 406 93 54 / 93 406 93 23

🕓 *Wed.–Fri. 11am–2pm, 3.30pm–7pm; Sat., Sun. and public holidays 11am–8pm* ● *500 Ptas*

Designed by Norman Foster, this gigantic communications tower started operating just before the Olympic Games in 1992. A viewing-platform has been installed on the tenth floor, 1,800 ft above sea level.

Not forgetting

■ **Museu de la Ciència (58)** Carrer Teodor Roviralta, 55 - 08022 ☎ 93 212 60 50 🕓 Tue.–Sun. and public holidays 10am–8pm ● 500 Ptas; first Sunday of the month free *The Science Museum, which occupies a Modernist building dating from 1910, offers a planetarium, permanent interactive displays, film screenings, temporary exhibitions and lectures. It also includes an astronomical observatory.* ■ **Jardins de la Tamarita (59)** Passeig Sant Gervasi, 47/49 - 08022 🕓 summer 10am–8pm; winter 10am–6pm ● free *A private park occupying over one acre, designed in a Romantic style at the turn of the century by the landscape gardener Nicolau Maria Rubió i Tudurí. It was bought by the City Hall in 1993 and the gardens are now open to the public.*

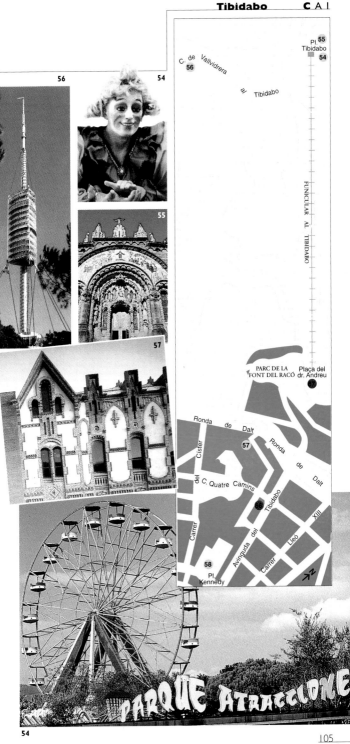

56

54

55

57

54

PI **55**
Tibidabo
54

C. de Vallvidrera **56**

al   Tibidabo

FUNICULAR AL TIBIDABO

PARC DE LA
FONT DEL RACÓ
Plaça del
dr. Andreu

Ronda   de   Dalt

Cister

57

Ronda

de

Dalt

del   C. Quatre Camins

Carrer

Avinguda del   Tibidabo

58

Lleó

XIII

Carrer

58
PI.
Kennedy

PARQUE ATRACCIONE

54

The Catalan sea coast

A whole host of beaches along the coasts to the north and south of Barcelona are easy to get to by train (lines C1 and C2 of RENFE ☎ 93 490 02 02).
The locals' favorites are those of Vilanova and Geltrú (30 miles to the south).

Further afield

For animal lovers

*Marineland Carretera del Malgrat,
Palafolls - 080389* ☎ *93 765 48 02*
3 miles south of Blanes
Aquatic park and dolphinarium. Other
attractions include parrots and birds of
prey.

Days out

THE INSIDER'S FAVORITES

Take a dip ... in the heart of the city

Barcelona is proud of its 2½ miles of beach, easily reached by public
transport and superbly equipped. To the south of the Olympic Port there
are the beaches of Sant Sebastià and Barceloneta 🔲 *10, 17, 36, 39, 41, 45,
57, 59, 64.* To the north lie the beaches of Nova Icària, Bogatell, Mar Bella
and Nova Mar Bella. 🔲 *6, 10, 36, 41, 45, 59, 141.* Nude bathing is
permitted in some parts of the beaches of Sant Sebastià and Mar Bella.

The famous Costa Brava, with its precipitous cliffs, unspoiled creeks and long beaches, has attracted tourists ever since the 19th century; the Costa Daurada is less well known, but also offers miles of white sand; the Penedès region is dotted with the vineyards which produce the internationally renowned cava; the stark beauty and artistic treasures of

Further afield

Montserrat (1–4)

37 miles west of Barcelona

🚆 From Carrer Viriat, near Sants station, at 9am, round trip at 5pm (6pm in July and Aug.). Journey time 1 hr 15 mins

● Round trip, Mon.–Sat. 2,420 Ptas; Sun. 2,760 Ptas

🚆 From Ferrocarrils de la Generalitat (FGC) station, Plaça Espanya, line R-5, journey time 1 hr 15 mins. Get off at Montserrat Aeri station and take the cable car

● Round trip, 2,290 Ptas

🚌 Several roads lead to Montserrat. Only one route is free: the motorway N11 to Martorell, then the local C1411 to Montserrat

Tourist office
Plaça de la Creu - 08199 Montserrat
☎ 93 835 02 01
➡ 93 835 06 59

Vilafranca del Penedès (5)

34 miles west of Barcelona

🚆 From Carrer Joan Güell, on the corner of Carrer Europa (behind the Corte Inglés Diagonal), journey time 55 mins

● Round trip 1,180 Ptas

🚆 From Plaça Catalunya, Sants, Arc de Triomf, Sant

108

Montserrat, the spiritual heart of Catalonia, are overwhelming … These are just some of the excursions available from the Catalan capital, and they all provide an opportunity to explore a region proud of its history, traditions and language.

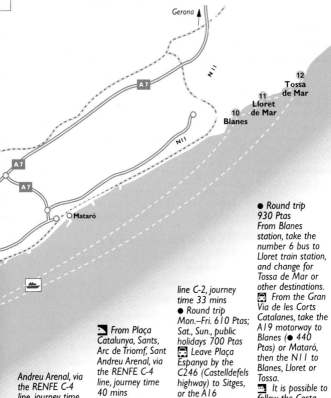

Andreu Arenal, via the RENFE C-4 line, journey time 52 mins
● Round trip Mon.–Fri. 730 Ptas; Sat., Sun., public holidays 850 Ptas
🚗 Take the A7 motorway to Vilafranca (● 385 Ptas), or to Molins de Rei, then the N340

Tourist office
Carrer Cort, 12 - 08720 Vilafranca
☎ 93 892 03 58

S. Sadurní d'Anoia (6)

25 miles west of Barcelona
🚆 From Carrer Comte d'Urgell (corner of Carrer Paris), journey time 45 mins
● Round trip 425 Ptas

🚆 From Plaça Catalunya, Sants, Arc de Triomf, Sant Andreu Arenal, via the RENFE C-4 line, journey time 40 mins
● Round trip Mon.–Fri. 700 Ptas; Sat., Sun., public holidays 800 Ptas
🚗 Take the A7 motorway to S. Sadurní (● 370 Ptas)

Tourist office
Pl. del Ajuntament, 1 - 08770 S. Sadurní
☎ 93 891 03 25

Sitges (7-9)

36 miles southwest of Barcelona
🚆 From Ronda Universitat, 33, journey time 50 mins
● Round trip 850 Ptas
🚆 From Passeig de Gràcia, Sants, Clot, Sant Andreu Comtal via RENFE line C-2, journey time 33 mins
● Round trip Mon.–Fri. 610 Ptas; Sat., Sun., public holidays 700 Ptas
🚗 Leave Plaça Espanya by the C246 (Castelldefels highway) to Sitges, or the A16 motorway to Sitges (● 620 ptas)

Tourist office
Sínia Morera, 1 - 08870 Sitges
☎ 93 894 42 51
➡ 93 894 43 05

Blanes (10) Lloret (11) Tossa (12)

41, 42 and 49 miles north of Barcelona
🚆 From Estació de Nord, journey time 1 hr 10 mins
● Round trip 1,250 Ptas
🚆 From Sants, Plaça de Catalunya, Arc de Triomf and El Clot-Aragó, via the RENFE C-1 line, journey time 1 hr 20 mins

● Round trip 930 Ptas
From Blanes station, take the number 6 bus to Lloret train station, and change for Tossa de Mar or other destinations.
🚗 From the Gran Via de les Corts Catalanes, take the A19 motorway to Blanes (● 440 Ptas) or Mataró, then the N11 to Blanes, Lloret or Tossa.
🚢 It is possible to follow the Costa Brava by boat, from Blanes to Tossa. You can make stops without paying extra (● 1,200 Ptas). Boat trips to view the depths of the sea are also organized (☎ 972342229)

Tourist Offices
Blanes
Pl. de Catalunya, 21 - 17300 Blanes
☎ 97 233 03 48
➡ 97 233 46 86

Lloret de Mar
Plaça de la Vila, 1 - 17310 Lloret
☎ 91 236 47 35
➡ 97 236 77 50

Tossa de Mar
Av. del Pelegri, 25 - 17320 Tossa
☎ 97 234 01 08
➡ 97 234 07 12

Montserrat is a spectacular mountain, with granite rocks which have been sculpted by the passing of time to endow them with strange and enchanting forms. It provides the setting for a Benedictine monastery, where pilgrims come to worship the black Virgin. About two million visitors annually pass through the spiritual heart of Catalonia.

Further afield

Monestir de Montserrat (1)

🕐 **Masses** 7.30am–7.30pm **Virgin's chapel** 8–10.30am, noon–6.30pm **Children's choir** 1pm, 7.10pm (except July and Christmas holidays) 🍴 🍸 ⛲ 🏂

The Benedictine presence in Montserrat dates from 1025. The most important building in the present monastery is the basilica; consecrated in 1592, it has a single nave, rounded Gothic arches and six chapels on each side. Outstanding among the later additions are the neo-Romanesque apse, with the cupola and façade finished off with sculptures by the Vallmitajana brothers (1900–1). The 12th-century statue of the patron of Catalonia, the black Virgin affectionately known as the 'Moreneta', is venerated behind the altar, in a little chapel decorated with mosaics by Josep Obiols and bas-reliefs by Joaquim Roa.

Muséu de Montserrat (2)

🕐 Mon.–Fri. 10am–6pm; Sat. and public holidays 9.30am–6.30pm ● 500 Ptas; free for under-10s

This is divided into five sections: archeology from the Biblical Orient; gold plate and liturgical objects (15th–20th centuries); paintings from the 16th–18th centuries (including works by P. Berruguete, El Greco, Caravaggio, Luca Giordano and Tiepolo); modern painting and sculpture (by, among others, Pissarro, Degas, Sisley, Monet, Rusiñol, Dalí and Picasso), and 'Nigra Sum', given over to the iconography of Montserrat. There are also temporary exhibitions.

Viewing-platform and monumental rosary (3)

Two cable-car railroads provide access to the buildings lodged in the mountain, some distance from the monastery. One of them leads to the cave, known as the Santa Cova, where, according to tradition, the black Virgin was found. In this very same grotto the founder of the Jesuits, Ignacio de Loyola, started to write his 'Spiritual Exercises' in the 16th century. From there, it is possible to follow, by walking along a craggy path, the stages of a monumental rosary, consisting of fifteen sculptural groups realized by artists such as Gaudí and Limona. The Sant Joan railroad climbs to a height of 3,300 ft, with a gradient of 65.5%, and after that the chapel of Sant Miquel and that of Sant Jeroni, Romanesque in style, can be reached after walking for 50 and 60 minutes, respectively.

Cueva de Salnitre (4)
Collbató, 3 miles from the station ☎ 93 777 03 09

Montserrat stretches for over 6 miles; its highest point is the peak of Sant Jeroni (4,015 ft). The presence of a sea which covered the territory of present-day Catalonia in the tertiary era explains the characteristics of this relief. Montserrat was originally a mountain range comparable to the Pyrenees, but gradual erosion has bequeathed it the astonishing features visible today. Of the countless caverns nestling inside the mountain, the best known is the Cova de Salnitre, 1,800 ft long.

Not forgetting

■ **Montserrat** Plaça de los Apòstols - 08199 Montserrat. *This restaurant also has a self-service section. Wonderful view.*

2

The great plain of Penedès is the wine-growing heartland of Catalonia: in 1998 the grape harvest topped the 220,000 ton mark, and more than 3½ million gallons of wine were produced, a large part being 'cava', the renowned Catalan champagne. In festivals extending from spring to fall, the squares of Penedès are turned into stages for the fascinating

Further afield

Vilafranca del Penedès (4)

Originally a Roman town, Vilafranca del Penedès is the capital of the 'comarca' (county) of Alt Penedès. This region is now an important commercial, agricultural and wine-making center, but it still preserves some distinctive features of its rich past. In the Middle Ages the fairs and markets of Vilafranca were very famous, and these days the Festa Major, on August 30, the day of its patron saint, Saint Felix, is one of the most well-known festivals in the whole of Catalonia. **The Plaça Jaume I (a)**, the heart of the city, is the site of the royal palace, the **Palau del Comtes-Reis (b)**, a beautiful example of Romanesque-Gothic architecture (12th–13th centuries), which was the scene of the death of King Peter II, or Peter the Great, on November 11, 1285. Since 1934 the palace has housed the Museu de Vilafranca, in which the **Museu del Vi (c)**, the only one of its kind in Spain, is the most interesting section. It offers a very informative survey of the history of vines and wine, and it includes an art gallery, a collection of *porrons* (carafes with a large conical spout) and a wonderful selection of the glasses used by wine tasters. Just opposite the royal palace, the **Basilica de Santa Maria (d)**, begun in 1285, is a model of Catalan Gothic at its purest, despite its neo-Gothic façade.

Sant Sadurní d'Anoia (5)

Sant Sadurní d'Anoia is considered the capital of the famous Catalan champagne, 'cava', with Codorniu and Freixenet undoubtedly being the most renowned producers. **Caves Codorniu (e)** is one of the biggest wine-makers in the world: its premises are spread over five levels and a total length of some 18 miles, and they are equipped to handle around one hundred million bottles. The oldest building, designed by the Modernist architect Josep Puig i Cadafalch at the end of the 19th century, has been declared a national monument. Its polychromic glass canopies, with its vaults divided by spectacular parabolic brick-work arches, give it the air of a cathedral. Every year the factory attracts 200,000 visitors. **Caves Freixenet (f)** owes its name to the property La Freixeneda, the birthplace of the company's founder, Pere Ferrer i Bosch. The vineyard was established at the end of the 19th century and, despite subsequent refurbishments and enlargements, has preserved its original façade. In the entrance a mural reproduces an extremely popular poster, depicting a little red-headed boy cradling a bottle in his arms. The image, commissioned by Pere Ferrer to mark the International Exhibition in 1929, has become a classic of Spanish advertising. **Mon del Cava (g)**, the legendary shop at number 1 in Carrer Pau Casals, sells all types of products for both professional connoisseurs and enthusiasts.

Not forgetting

■ **Cal Figarot** Carrer General Prim, 11 - 08720 Vilafranca del Penedès ☎ 93 817 05 42 *A Modernist building, the headquarters of the* castellers *of Vilafranca, who rehearse there every Friday evening. With a bar which serves tapas and local specialties.* ■ **Cal Ton** Carrer Casal, 8 - 08720 Vilafranca del Penedès ☎ 93 890 37 41 *Simple cooking which often borrows ideas from the new wave.*

spectacle of the *castells*, human towers of up to ten levels, formed by local residents in traditional costumes.

5c

5a

Vilafranca del Penedès is not just for **wine lovers** – the town also proudly displays its historic past.

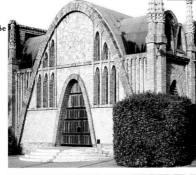

6e

5e

6e

With its elegant promenade, culminating in the 18th-century parish church of Sant Bartomeu and Santa Tecla, Sitges is a well-known beach resort. The sophisticated villas built by the 'Americans' (locals who returned after making their fortunes on the other side of the Atlantic) were an added attraction for the Modernists who moved here in the

Further afield

Casc Antic (6)

In the old town ('casc antic' in Catalan), elegant Modernist buildings rub shoulders with whitewashed fishermen's houses, most of which have been refurbished. Inland, the center is bounded by the Carrer Major and the Carrer Parellades, which has a wealth of offshoots, typical alleyways like the 'Carrer del Pecat' ('street of sin'), so-called because it is the setting for a somewhat uninhibited nightlife!

Museu Maricel de Mar and Museu Cau Ferrat (7)
Fonollar - 08870 ☎ 93 890 364 ➡ 93 894 85 29

🕐 Tue.–Fri. 9.30–2pm, 4pm–6pm; Sat. 9.30–2pm, 4pm–8pm; Sun 9.30–2pm
● 500 Ptas per museum; combined ticket with the Museu Romàntic, 800 Ptas; half price for senior citizens and groups; first Wednesday of the month free ◻ ⚅

The two museums, in adjoining buildings near the sea front, make up a single exhibition complex, although it is possible to visit only one. The **Museu Maricel**, the former residence of the American millionaire Charles Deering, has now been given over to Sitges and houses the Pérez Rosales endowment of beautiful Roman murals, the very fine 14th-century Sant Bartolomeu chapel and works from various periods before the Renaissance. Don't miss the panoramic view of the beach. At the start of the 20th century, the Modernist painter, poet and dramatist Santiago Rusiñol (1861–1931) acquired two fishermen's houses and set up his studio in them. They are now the centerpiece of the **Museu Cau Ferrat**, which exhibits the artist's works, along with *azulejos* (traditional wall tiles), Romanesque and Gothic sculptures and a collection of Catalan iron-work (*ferrat*, hence the museum's name) which Rusiñol collected ever since his youth. The artist brought in his wake other artists, such as the painters Ramon Casas and Picasso, the musicians Albéniz and Falla, and a host of others, thus turning Sitges into the Mecca of Modernism and a popular vacation spot for the bourgeoisie of Barcelona …

Museu Romàntic (8)
Sant Gaudenci 1 - 08870 ☎ 93 894 24 69

🕐 Tue.–Fri. 9.30–2pm, 4pm–6pm; Sat. 9.30–2pm, 4pm–8pm; Sun 9.30–2pm
● 500 Ptas per museum; combined ticket with the Museu Maricel and the Museu Cau Ferrat, 800 Ptas; half price for senior citizens and groups; first Wednesday of the month free ◻ 🗊 at all times.

This neoclassical residence is evidence of the wealth of those inhabitants who made their fortunes in Latin America (especially Cuba and Puerto Rico). A stroll through its richly decorated rooms affords a glimpse of middle-class Catalan life in the 19th century. A beautiful collection of antique dolls on the second floor.

Not forgetting

■ **El Velero** Passeig de la Ribera, 38 - 08870 ☎ 93 894 20 51 from Oct. 15 to Apr. 15, closed on Sun. evenings and Mon. *Typical local cuisine and a beautiful view of the sea.* ■ **Cal Pinxo** Passeig de la Ribera, 5 - 08870 ☎ 93 894 74 64 closed on Sun. evenings and Mon. *Excellent fish-based specialties.*

19th century in search of light and the sea.

Crystal-clear blue sea, idyllic panoramas, hidden coves, golden sandy beaches, untouched promontories, clumps of pines bordering on the sea shore. The coast of the province of Girona is a wonder of nature which can be explored on delightful, relaxing boat trips.

Further afield

Blanes (9)

The **chapel of La Esperança (a)**, which contains an interesting collection of sailors' *ex-votos*, provides a link with the seafaring past of this small port, which nowadays devotes its energy to tourism. Do not miss the opportunity to visit the **Jardí de Marimurtra (b)**, a botanical garden founded in 1921 by Karl Faust; set on a striking promontory which plunges into the Mediterranean, it extends over more than 40 acres. Only the small neoclassical temple is out of place in this sumptuous natural showcase. More than 4,000 species of plants from all over the world are on display here; the most remarkable collection is that of grasses coming from the arid regions of southern Africa and Central America. Some 3 miles from Blanes, on the way to Lloret, the **Jardí Pinya de Rosa (c)**, another attractive and interesting botanical garden, boasts the most beautiful collection in the world of Indian fig trees and Banyan trees, with aerial roots.

Lloret de Mar (10)

Tucked away in the long coastlines of Lloret are the most beautiful *cales* (coves) in the Mediterranean; they were so famous at one time that in the 19th century they were referred to in *Marina*, a famous *zarzuela* (type of operetta). They can be reached by road but it is advisable to approach them from the sea by taking advantage of the boats which leave Blanes, Lloret and Tossa and stop off at the *cales*. The loveliest ones are, from East to West, Cala Canyelles (f.p.), **Cala Banys (d)**, **Cala Fenals (e)**, Cala Santa Cristina (f.p.) – with a chapel – and Cala Boadella (f.p.) – with a beach for nude bathing: so there is something for everybody! In summer one can visit (by appointment with the tourist office) the Santa Clotilde, on the outskirts of Lloret. In the town itself, the Modernist-style **chapel of the Sagrament (f)**, in Carrer de la Vila, is worth a visit, as is the **Museu Can Garriga (g)**, on Passeig Camprodon i Arrieta, which exhibits work by local painters, models of boats and photographs: this museum occupies the former residence of an 'American', a local who made good after emigrating.

Tossa de Mar (11)

La Vila Vella (h), the old town, perched on its picturesque promontory, is the only surviving example of a fortified medieval village on the Catalan coast. The **town walls (i)** were built 800 years ago, and have now been classified as a national monument. An imposing building houses the **Museu Municipal (j)**, the first contemporary art museum in the whole of Spain. It displays works by artists who have known and loved Tossa, the most famous being Chagall, who considered this Catalan town 'a blue paradise'. Recently a **monument to Ava Gardner (m)** has been erected in the Vila Vella: in the 1950s the great star acted in a famous Hollywood film, *Pandora*, which made the name of this Catalan town known all over the world.

Not forgetting

■ **Las Petxines** Pg. Verdaguer, 16 - 17320 Lloret ☎ 97 236 41 37 ▣ open from Mar. 29 to Nov. 18; closed on Mon ■ **Castell Vell** Pg. Roig i Soler, 2 - 17320 Tossa ☎ 97 234 10 30 ▣ 💈

Shopping hours

Generally speaking, stores in Barcelona open from 10am to 1.30 or 2pm, and from 4.30 or 5pm to 8pm. Many close on Saturday afternoons, especially if they are not near the main shopping streets. In December shops also open on Sundays.

Where to shop

Sales

Do not miss out on the bargains in the two annual sales: the *rebaixes d'hivern* (January–February) and the *rebaixes d'estiu* (July–August).

The shopping route

The most outstanding stores are concentrated on the axis following the Rambla–Passeig de Gràcia–Avinguda Diagonal. The entire route is served by the distinctive blue *TombBus*.

66 Shops

THE INSIDER'S FAVORITES

What to buy?

The city's commercial traditions, stretching back centuries, are still very much in evidence today. Its countless and impressive stores are still one of its main attractions. Avant-garde furniture and accessories, fresh food or culinary delicacies, pottery, craft goods … All these, and more, can be found here, and always of the highest quality.

INDEX BY SUBJECT

Barcelona has the ultimate in small shops which have stayed in the hands of a single family for over a century ... However, department stores have also been on the scene for several decades: the first, and best known, the Corte Inglés, has four branches in Barcelona. The 1990s have seen the addition of shopping malls such as Maremagnum, the Illa

➡ Where to shop

El Corte Inglés (1)

Plaça de Catalunya, 14 - 08002 ☎ 93 306 38 00/93 266 01 01
➡ 933176232

Ⓜ *Catalunya, Urquinaona* **Clothes, perfumes, accessories and food**
◗ *Mon.–Sat. 10am–9.30pm* ▣ 🍴 ▨ ▣ ◑ *Portal de l'Àngel, 19/21 - 08002*
☎ *93 306 38 00; Avinguda Diagonal, 471 - 08036 ☎ 93 419 20 20 ;Avinguda
Diagonal, 617 - 08028 ☎ 93 419 28 28*

The Corte Inglés is the most important Spanish chain, and it also owns supermarkets and travel agencies. The Plaça Catalunya branch, one of the city's favorite meeting places, looks like an Art Deco liner: it is spread over several floors and offers a vast array of products: clothes for men, women and children, perfumes, accessories and gifts, home furnishings, electro-domestic goods, garden articles, food ... and even more! Close to this enormous shopping center, the building on the Avinguda Portal de l'Àngel stocks office accessories, records, books, photographic material, sports articles, computers, video and hi-fi equipment and gifts. The staff is always extremely helpful and knowledgeable ...

El Triangle (2)

Plaça de Catalunya- Carrer Pelai- Carrer Bergara - 08002
☎ 93 318 01 08 ➡ 93 412 53 76

Ⓜ *Catalunya, Universitat* **Books, games, furniture, perfumes, clothes and
accessories** ◗ *Mon.–Sat. 10am–10pm* ▣ ▨ ▣

The Triangle is Barcelona's newest shopping mall, with large and small stores side by side, most of them selling ready-to-wear clothing with Spanish or foreign labels. Four large stores have pride of place: FNAC (books and records), Habitat (household goods), Sephora (perfumes) and Grand Optical (spectacles).

Diagonal and, most recently, the Triangle in Plaça Catalunya.

L'Illa (3)
Avinguda Diagonal, 557 - ☎ 93 444 00 00 ➡ 93 444 00 08

Ⓜ *Maria Cristina* **Books, games, food and sports articles** Ⓢ *Mon.–Sat. 10am–9pm* 🟦 🟦 🟦 🟦

L'Illa occupies a huge building, put up by the architect Rafael Moneo in the beginning of the 1990s. Its imposing façade is the longest in Barcelona (436 ft). This vast shopping mall contains 133 stores, including branches of international chains like Marks & Spencer and Decathlon.

Maremagnum (4)
Moll d'Espanya, Port Vell - 08003 ☎ 93 225 81 00 ➡ 93 412 53 76

Ⓜ *Drassanes, Barceloneta* **Gifts, clothes and accessories** Ⓢ *daily 11am–11pm* 🟦 🟦 🟦 🟦

Maremagnum, in the heart of the Port Vell, the city's new seafront, connected to the Rambla by a bridge over the sea, is a favorite spot for a stroll on Sundays; with its 50 stores, fast-food joints, bars and restaurants, you can combine shopping and relaxation under one roof …

In the area

Hidden within the winding medieval alleyways around this square are the oldest and most original shops in the whole of Barcelona. Sometimes time seems to have stood still here. It is always worthwhile exploring here for unusual souvenirs and gifts.

Where to shop

El Ingenio (5)
Carrer Rauric, 6 - 08002 ☎ 933177138 ➡ 933010095

M *Liceu* **Theater properties, masks and magic tricks** 🕐 *Mon.–Fri. 10am–1.30pm, 4.15–8pm; Sat. 10am–2pm, 5pm–8.30pm* ⬛

Founded in 1838, this store specializes in theatrical goods, and a whole host of companies do their shopping here! Even Salvador Dalí was a regular ... El Ingenio allows the public into its workshop, to see the manufacturing process of the *gegants* and the *caps-gros*, the giant puppets which traditionally parade the streets on Catalan holidays. On display there are Carnival masks, games and magic tricks for special occasions ... and, once a week, the store puts on its own magic show.

Herboristeria del Rei (6)
Carrer Vidre, I - 08002 ☎ ➡ 933180512

M *Liceu* **Medicinal plants** 🕐 *Mon.–Sat. 10am–2pm, 5–8pm* ⬛

This extraordinary herbalist's shop, run by the same family ever since it opened in 1823, was granted the official title of 'Suppliers of the Royal Household' in the middle of the 19th century. Situated in an astonishing backstreet which opens on to the arches of the Plaça Reial, it has preserved its original furnishings, designed by the famous theater designer Soler i Rovirosa. The shop is dominated by a monument to the naturalist Linnaeus, a fountain created by the Baratta brothers. Its shelves are lined with a huge array of herbs, spices and teas, along with candles, natural perfumes and oils for massages.

La Manual Alpargatera (7)
Carrer Avinyó, 7 - 08002 ☎ 933010172 ➡ 933011829

M *Liceu* **Hand-made shoes** 🕐 *Mon.–Fri. 9.30am–1.30pm, 4.30–8pm; Sat. 10am–1.30pm, 4–8pm* ⬛

Although the shop produces and sells traditional footwear, from Catalonia or other parts of Spain, it stocks more modern styles too, also made using traditional methods. There is no doubt that all their shoes are of the highest quality – they boast of being the official suppliers to the Vatican – and made by hand – the workshop is on the premises!

Cereria Subirà (8)
Baixada Llibreteria, 7 - 08002 ☎ 933152606 ➡ 933103733

M *Liceu* **Candles** 🕐 *Mon.–Fri. 9am–1.30pm, 4–7.30pm; Sat. 9am–1.30pm* ⬛

Founded in 1761, this shop, with its highly formal turn-of-the-century décor, is the oldest in Barcelona. The candles, whether religious or decorative, are lovingly arranged on the shelves, alongside enchanting knick-knacks. The home-made natural beeswax candles cover a wide range of styles, from the most traditional to the most modern design ... Reckon on spending between 3,000 and 10,000 Pesetas.

Not forgetting

⬛ **Sombrereria Obach (9)** Carrer Call, 2 - 08002 ☎ 933184094 *Hats of all kinds, from Catalan barretines to Italian Borsalinos.*

El Ingenio is an Aladdin's cave of theatrical goods and carnival masks!

In the area

Artisans, antique dealers and gallery owners have opted to set up shop in the narrow backstreets of Barcelona's old Jewish quarter, between the Plaça del Pi and the cathedral, in the heart of the Barri Gòtic. A quiet neighborhood, ideal for wandering about with no special aim, apart from

Where to shop

L'Arca de l'Àvia (10)
Carrer Banys Nous, 20 - 08002 ☎ 933021598

M *Liceu, Jaume I* **Antiques** 🕐 *Mon.–Fri. 10.30am–2pm, 5–8pm; Sat. 10.30–2pm* ▭

This shop was opened in 1840 by a family of lace-makers and importers, at that time the official supplier for the Spanish Royal household. Their descendants have kept the business going, and these days the proprietors of the Arca de l'Àvia buy and sell fabric, old and modern Catalan bobbin lace, period dolls, silk, hope-chests and small pieces of furniture. The merchandise is displayed with exquisite taste inside the shop, conjuring up a fairy-tale atmosphere. The owners also have a shop in Maó, in Menorca, one of the Balearic Islands.

Gemma Povo (11)
Carrer Banys Nous, 5 - 08002 ☎ 933013476 ➡ 933180144

M *Liceu, Jaume I* **Wrought-iron articles** 🕐 *Mon.–Fri. 10am–1.30pm, 4.30–8pm; Sat. 10am–1.30pm, 5–8.30pm* ▭

Ferran Povo, a specialist in wrought-iron work, first opened a shop in the 1950s. Now his daughter Gemma is continuing the family tradition and, while still drawing on the motifs created by her father, has managed to update it. In her friendly shop, which is spread over several rooms, she displays some old items, often incorporated into newer works, as well as small pieces of furniture, such as lamps, tables and bedsteads.

Casa Miranda (12)
Carrer Banys Nous, 15 - 08002 ☎ ➡ 933018329

M *Liceu, Jaume I* **Hand-made wickerwork** 🕐 *Mon.–Sat. 9.30am–2pm, 4.30pm–8pm* ▭

Two hundred years of experience in the wickerwork business have made Casa Miranda not only one of the most famous crafts shops in Barcelona, but also one of the most prestigious in the whole of Spain. This family of wickerworkers makes and repairs all kinds of chairs, from the simplest to the most sophisticated, such as rocking chairs. If you have trouble fitting these into your suitcase, take a look at the specialties of the house – lamps, cradles and other small pieces of furniture.

Coses de Casa (13)
Plaza de Sant Josep Oriol, 5 - 08002 ☎ ➡ 933027328

M *Liceu, Jaume I* **Household fabrics** 🕐 *Mon.–Fri. 10am–2pm, 4.30–8pm; Sat. 10am–2pm, 5–8.30pm* ▭

Behind its multicolored windows, Coses de Casa offers a vast range of table linen, sheets, bed-covers, drapes and other household fabrics, sold by the meter. There is a great variety of designs, which combine tradition and modernity, and a beautiful selection of *llengua mallorquina*, a printed fabric derived from the largest of the Balearic islands, which is used for drapes and tablecloths. Its sparkling interplay of golden yellow and coral-red is guaranteed to brighten up any interior.

pleasure to the eyes and perhaps an unexpected purchase.

In the area

Between the Plaça del Pi and the cathedral the narrow streets of the Barri Gòtic seem to get wider, as if making room for an ever-larger crowd, attracted by the number and variety of the shops. This

 # Where to shop

Fargas (14)
Carrer Boters, 2 - 08002 ☎ 933020342 ➡ 934125805

Ⓜ *Jaume I, Liceu* **Chocolates and sweetmeats** 🕐 *Mon.–Fri. 9am–1.30pm, 4–8pm; Sat. 9.30am–2pm, 4–8pm* ▣

Ever since 1827, the same family has been preparing chocolates, sweetmeats and *turrons* (nougats) of all kinds. Fargas also roasts its own coffee and presents a vast range of traditional delicacies and candies. Neither the exterior nor the interior decoration have been changed since the shop opened: you can still even see a beautifully preserved old cocoa millstone, which was once driven by a mule.

Àngel Batlle (15)
Carrer Palla, 23 - 08002 ☎ 933015884

Ⓜ *Jaume I, Liceu* **Old books** 🕐 *Mon.–Sat. 9am–1.30pm, 4–7.30pm* ▣

All four walls of this shop, founded in 1900, are completely covered with old bookshelves groaning with works of literature, history and art history, along with period prints. The Batlle bookshop regularly publishes catalogs, and all its titles can be ordered by mail.

La Pineda (16)
Carrer del Pi, 16 - 08002 ☎ 933024393

Ⓜ *Jaume I, Liceu* **Food, wines** 🕐 *Mon.–Sat. 9am–1pm, 5–10pm; Sun. and public holidays 11am–1pm, 7–10pm* ▣

Since this shop opened in 1930 it has specialized in charcuterie (cold meats), cheese and wine. The produce can be bought to take out, but it is also possible to eat it *in situ*, in a zone which is an exact copy of an old grocery store. There is a veritable forest of hams hanging from the ceiling, and the glass-fronted cabinets on the back wall are the setting for the greatest treasure of all: its wonderful collection of wines. Specialties from all over Spain are available here, from succulent hams from Salamanca and Jabugo to *chorizo* (salami) from Soria, or from *fuet* (black sausage) from Vic to white sausage from Pallars, or from exceptional cheeses from La Mancha and Galicia to wines from La Rioja, Penedès and the Ribera del Duero.

M. Messegué (17)
Carrer del Pi, 13 - 08002 ☎ 933011334

Ⓜ *Jaume I, Liceu* **Herbalists** 🕐 *Mon.–Sat. 10am–1.30pm, 4.30–8pm* ▣ ▥
Carrer Sepúlveda, 123 - 08014; Carrer Olzinelles, 19 bis - 08014

Plants and natural cosmetics with the Messegué brand name. The store's specialties include royal jelly and herbs for circulatory conditions.

Not forgetting

■ **Artur Ramon (18)** Carrer de la Palla, 25 - 08002 ☎ 933025970 ➡ 933182833 *Antique shop specializing in works of art (paintings, sculptures and drawings). Next door there is an art gallery.*

neighborhood is a favorite of gourmets, because it is endowed with some outstanding food stores.

BOMBONES

In the area

The area around the Plaça del Pi and the Plaça Sant Josep Oriol comprises one of the most lively shopping zones in the Barri Gòtic. Trendy stores rub shoulders with more traditional establishments, and cafés, pastry-shops and craft workshops turn out to have some unlikely neighbors.

Where to shop

Beardsley (19)

Carrer Petritxol, 12 - 08002 ☎ 93 301 05 75 ➡ 93 302 71 23

Ⓜ Liceu **Antiques, office and household goods** 🕐 *Mon.–Fri. 9.30am–1.30pm, 4.30–8pm; Sat. 10am–2pm, 5–8.30pm* ▣ 🖼 *Carrer Cardenal Cassanyes, 7 - 08002* **Photographs and frames**

More than a mere shop, Beardsley is a veritable bazaar, a hotchpotch of antiques of all kinds: small pieces of furniture, candelabras and table articles. In the basement, the stationery section has a wide range of gifts and, at Carnival time, masks and other accessories.

Estamperia d'Art – Artigues Editor (20)

Plaça del Pi, 1 - 08002 ☎ 93 318 68 30

Ⓜ Liceu **Prints and lithographs** 🕐 *Mon.–Fri. 9.30am–1.30pm, 4.30–8pm; Sat. 10am–1.30pm, 5–8pm* ▣

Founded in 1789, and in the hands of the same family ever since, this small shop is the only one in Spain which sells, and sometimes publishes, reproductions of works of art from museums from all over the world. It also stocks lithographs of the most famous old masters, and will frame them for you too.

Ganiveteria Roca (21)

Plaça del Pi, 3 - 08002 ☎ 93 302 12 41 ➡ 93 412 53 49

Ⓜ Liceu **Razors, knives and scissors** 🕐 *Mon.–Fri. 9.45am–1.30pm, 4.15–8pm; Sat. 10am–2pm, 5–8pm* ▣

Ever since 1911 this wonderful cutler's shop, decorated in a Modernist style, with influences from Eastern Europe, has been selling products from all the big international manufacturers. On display round the anvil which dominates the interior are collectors' items and reproductions of old pieces. A small but important touch: the after-sale service is outstanding.

Caelum (22)

Carrer Palla, 8 - 08002 ☎ 93 302 69 93

Ⓜ Liceu, Jaume I **Products made in convents** 🕐 *Mon.–Sat. 10.30am–2pm, 5–8.30pm; Sun. 10.30am–2pm* ▣

A truly bizarre shop on the site of the old thermal baths. It only sells produce made in Spanish convents and monasteries: delicious sweetmeats from the Clare nuns of Alcalá de Guadaira in Seville; cherries in liqueur from Rosal de Pontevedra; exquisite chocolates from Berga, near Barcelona; spiced wine from the *Santes Creus* of Tarragona; exceptional cheese from the Roncesvalles monastery in Navarra, and *Amarguillos* (bitter almond pastries) from the Dominican nuns of Toro in Zamora.

Not forgetting

■ **Joguines Montforte (23)** Plaça Sant Josep Oriol, 3 - 08002 ☎ ➡ 93 318 22 85 *Founded in 1840, this shop specializes in parlor games and accessories for pool.* ■ **Molsa (24)** Plaça Sant Josep Oriol, 1 - 08002 ☎ 93 302 31 03 ➡ 93 412 79 08 *Popular Spanish and Catalan pottery, hand-painted glass and souvenirs.*

22

At Molsa the humble souvenir becomes a work of art. A huge selection to satisfy even the most demanding customer.

In the area

The narrow streets in the Ribera neighborhood, which stretches between the Santa Maria del Mar church and the Born, the old central market, are the setting for crafts workshops, artists' studios, art galleries and museums. Restaurants, bars and traditional stores all enhance the

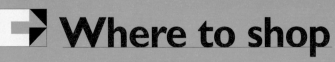

Where to shop

Ici et là (25)
Plaça Santa Maria, 2 - 08003 ☎ ➡ 93 268 11 67

Ⓜ Jaume I **Household articles** 🕙 Mon. 4.30–8.30pm; Tue.–Sat. 10.30am–2.30pm, 4.30–8.30pm ▣

Conceived as an art gallery, this sophisticated store presents the work of young designers, with one-off pieces or small series, made to measure. The display includes lamps, furniture, fabrics, bed covers, carpets and paintings, complemented by original articles from Africa: in fact, none of the stock is obtained through the traditional import-export networks. Ici et là also has branches in Paris, where there is an office which coordinates with the artists, and in San Francisco, where an on-line catalog has been compiled (www.icietla.com).

El Aleph (26)
Carrer Vigatans, 11 - 08003 ☎ ➡ 93 319 24 26

Ⓜ Jaume I **Glass objects** 🕙 Mon.–Sat. 10am–2pm, 4–8pm ▣

This recently opened workshop-showroom not only exhibits and sells, but also produces objects made by 'fusing' – melting glass and then shaping the resulting paste and combining it with others in different colors. The building's old vaulted cellars have been preserved, and the modern additions, such as a wooden staircase leading up to the store, workshop and exhibition space, are a perfect complement to their old-world charm. The Aleph not only sells items such as glass mobiles and large stained glass windows, made to order, but also small objects (earrings, necklaces, ashtrays …).

Casa Gispert (27)
Carrer Sombrerers, 23 - 08003 ☎ 93 319 75 35

Ⓜ Jaume I **Dried fruit, coffee and spices** 🕙 Mon.–Fri. 9am–1.30pm, 4–7.30pm; Sat. 10am–2pm, 5–8pm ▣

The Casa Gispert, a shop which has remained unchanged since it was founded in 1851, has long since shown its mastery of the art of coffee-roasting, but it also sells spices, chocolate, cocoa, mushrooms and an enormous range of dried fruit. The aromas and scents conjure up faraway lands, and the top-quality products are made with a respect for bygone traditions, in a warm and friendly atmosphere.

Tienda del Museu Tèxtil i de la Indumentària (28)
Carrer Montcada, 12 - 08003 ☎ 93 268 25 98

Ⓜ Jaume I **Clothes and accessories** 🕙 Tue.–Sat. 10am–8.30pm; Sun. 10am–3pm ▣ ▣ ▣

This store is next to the important textile museum ➡ 88. It contains all sorts of products connected with the wonderful world of fabrics: clothes, bags, shoes, cushions, sheets, ties, jewelry … All the pieces are designed by Spanish artists in general, and Catalan artists in particular: Antoni Miró and David Valls, for example, have contributed clothes, while Duch Claramunt and Ricardo Domingo have created jewelry. The store also sells fashion magazines and books.

colorful and vibrant Bohemian
atmosphere.

Via Laietana

M

Jaume I

Carrer de la Princesa

Carrer Vigatans

26

Carrer Barra de Ferro

Argenteria

9

Carrer Grunyi

Carrer Brosoli

Carrer dels Mirallers

Carrer dels Banys Vells

Carrer de Montcada

28 8
9   11
3

Pl. de Santa Maria

12

Carrer Sombrerers

27

C. Mosques

2

25

C. Espaseria   Carrer de Sta. Maria

Pg. del Born

25

27

26

The Rambla is Barcelona's main thoroughfare and busiest avenue, buzzing with life 24 hours a day. Some sections are named after the products on sale in the market stalls or booths (flowers, birds, books …).

Where to shop

Flors Carolina (29)
La Rambla, 10 (central boulevard) - 08002 ☎ 93 302 30 28

M *Liceu* **Flowers** 🕐 *Mon.–Sat. 7am–8pm; Sun. and public holidays 7am–2pm* ▭

One of the flower stalls opposite the Boqueria stands out from the rest through both its structure and its history: it is the property of a very old Catalan family, which has been selling flowers since 1888. Its sign-board pays homage to the family and summarizes an era spanning three generations: Carolina is the name not only of the grandmother who started the business, but also of her daughter and her granddaughter, who have perpetuated the tradition! They have become so popular that Barcelona has awarded them its Gold Medal. The flower arrangements of Flors Carolina, famous for their great refinement, are prepared in front of their customers' eyes … and it is not uncommon for local passers-by to stop just to watch the florists practicing their art. Their decorations for table centers are particularly stunning.

Escribà (30)
La Rambla, 83 - 08002 ☎ 93 301 60 27

M *Liceu* **Pastries, chocolates** 🕐 *daily 8.30am–9pm* ▭ 🍸 🍴 *Gran Via, 546 - 08011 ☎ 934547535; Avinguda Litoral, 42 - 08013 ☎ 932210729*

It is impossible to pass this shop without admiring the Modernist mosaics and stained glass windows of the façade. The sign over the door still reads 'Antigua Casa Figueras', the name of the grocery which occupied the store before the arrival in 1906 of the Escribà family and their delicious chocolates. Once its customers can manage to tear their eyes away from the extraordinary chocolate sculptures of Antoni Escribà, they can also appreciate the mouth-watering home-made pastries – especially the smaller tidbits – which they can eat in a recess within the shop itself.

Casa Beethoven (31)
La Rambla, 97 - 08002 ☎ 93 301 48 26 ➡ 93 302 72 96

M *Liceu* **Sheet music, music books** 🕐 *Mon.–Fri. 9am–8pm; Sat. 9am–1.30pm, 5–8pm* ▭

This shop, founded in 1915, is gloomy and narrow – though it seems to go on forever – yet it enjoys an international reputation! Its old wooden shelves strain under the weight of scores and books, mainly related to classical music, but with sections on flamenco, pop and rock … An essential port of call for music lovers in search of rare treasures.

El Indio (34)
Carrer del Carme, 24 - 08001 ☎ 93 317 54 42

M *Catalunya, Liceu* **Bazaar, household linen** 🕐 *Mon.–Sat. 10am–2pm, 4.30–8pm* 🔲

Nothing here seems to have changed since this shop opened in 1870, from the Modernist-style sign-board and windows to the interior decoration. Even the apparent disorder, the friendly and relaxed welcome of the staff, the smell of wood, the materials and aromas all seem to belong to another age … The stock covers a wide range of articles (mats, carpets, sheets …) at unbeatable prices.

In the area

It is said that anyone who drinks from the water fountain on Canaletes, the upper part of the Ramblas, is sure to return to Barcelona one day. One more reason to plunge into the very distinctive atmosphere of this neighborhood!

Where to shop

FNAC (33)
Plaça de Catalunya, 4 - 08002 ☎ 93 344 18 00 ➡ 93 344 18 01

🅼 *Catalunya, Passeig de Gràcia* **Books, records and videocassettes**
🕐 *Mon.–Sat. 10am–10pm* 🔲 🅿 🅷 *Avinguda Diagonal, 549-557 - 08029*
☎ *93 444 59 00*

At the time of the Olympic Games in 1992, the French chain FNAC opened a branch in Barcelona, in the Illa Diagonal shopping mall. At the end of 1998 it opened another inside an emblematic building, the Triangle, in Plaça Catalunya, in the heart of the city. Its huge expanse – some 75,000 sq. ft, spread over three floors – allows it to present not only a vast range of books and CDs, but also to set up sizeable computer and photographic departments and a small travel agency. There is also space for exhibitions, book signings and presentations, lectures and small-scale concerts.

Etnomusic (34)
Carrer Bonsuccés, 6 - 08001 ☎ 93 301 18 84

🅼 *Catalunya, Universitat* **Records** 🕐 *Mon.–Sat. 11am–8pm* 🔲

Who could imagine that all the world's music could fit into such a small space (500 sq. ft)? The answer lies with the Argentinean founder of Etnomusic, which acts as a magnet to the ever-growing crowd of world music fans from Barcelona and beyond, both through its tiny shop and its web site (www.etnomusic.com). Between these four walls, covered with posters, record sleeves, masks and CDs, you truly breath the air of distant lands! With its extensive catalog of 30,000 titles, the diminutive Etnomusic is really a heavyweight!

Antiga Casa Guarro (35)
Carrer Xuclà, 23 - 08001 ☎ 93 301 14 44 ➡ 93 414 49 33

🅼 *Liceu* **Herbs and medicinal plants** 🕐 *Mon.–Fri. 9am–2pm, 4–8pm; Sat. 9am–2pm, 5–8pm* 🔲

This herbalist's shop, founded in 1927, contains a vast array of herbs, medicinal plants and other natural health products. The Antiga Casa Garro is not only a very popular shop, with many loyal customers, but also an alternative medicine center: the store organizes courses and seminars on plants and their principal applications.

Not forgetting

■ **Llibreria Canuda (36)** Carrer Canuda, 4 - 08002 ☎ 93 302 10 35
This bookshop is treasure trove for art lovers. Your time – and patience! – may be rewarded by the discovery of a rarity, or some excellent bargains. Do not overlook the gallery at the rear of the shop, which puts on some interesting exhibitions.
■ **Discos Castelló (37)** Carrer Tallers 7 - 08001 ☎ 93 302 59 46
The latest sounds, curiosities, cut-price records, collectors' pieces … Fans of classical music, pop, rock, soul or jazz will all be satisfied: there really is something for everybody in the six shops scattered along the Carrer Tallers, just next to the Rambla.

The old meets the new: modern high street names rub shoulders with traditional retailers.

In the area

It is impossible to think of going shopping in Barcelona without a stroll down the Avinguda Portal de l'Àngel, one of the liveliest spots in town, where the shop windows sparkle with decorative lights and street performers entertain the continuous stream of passers-by.

# Where to shop

Villegas (38)
Carrer Comtal, 31 - 08002 ☎ 93 175 330 ➡ 93 317 24 93

Ⓜ *Catalunya* **Pottery** 🕐 *Mon.–Sat. 9.30am–2pm, 4–8.30pm* ▭

Señor Villegas is constantly reminding his customers that the pottery he sells in his shop is both original and hand-made. These customers comprise not only regulars, who buy either wholesale or retail, but also curious passers-by or astonished tourists … yet all are greeted with the same cordiality. If you are not in a hurry, get Señor Villegas to talk about the art of pottery, and some of his enthusiasm is bound to rub off on you.

Tomás Colomer (39)
Avinguda Portal de l'Àngel, 7 - 08002
☎ 93 301 55 22 ➡ 93 302 42 70

Ⓜ *Catalunya* **Jewelry, watches** 🕐 *Mon.–Sat. 9.30am–1.30pm, 4–8pm* ▭ ◀▶
Carrer Consell de Cent, 349 - 08007 ☎ 932156430

There is no doubt that this has one of the most beautiful shop windows on the entire avenue. Tomás Colomer, which opened in 1870, is the place to go if you are looking for products with a brand name created by top designers. Glamor and sophistication are the key words in this shop, although it is not elitist, as the owner does stock cheaper watches and gives the same attention to a customer looking for a set of luxury jewels as one who wants a simple necklace: both are asked to take a seat, so as to make the right choice …

Mil Barrets i Gorres (40)
Carrer Fontanella, 20 - 08010 ☎ 93 301 84 91 ➡ 93 318 16 18

Ⓜ *Catalunya* **Hats** 🕐 *Mon.–Sat. 9.30am–1.30pm, 4.30–8pm* ▭

An obligatory port of call for anybody who thinks that an elegant outfit is not complete without head-gear! Barcelona does not abound in hatters: only two or three are worth a detour. Mil Barrets i Gorres was founded in 1850 in Carrer Hospital, behind the Liceu Opera House – a favorite spot with the Catalan bourgeoisie – but moved to its present premises in Carrer Fontanella in 1917. The present owners have kept its traditions alive and love to regale their customers with tales of the famous Spanish personalities – sporting figures, actors and politicians – who have bought hats here … These precedents may be enough to convince you too!

Not forgetting

■ **Raima (41)** Carrer Comtal; 27 - 08002 ☎ 93 317 49 66 *Paper, on display in every shape, color and size imaginable, definitely rules the roost here. The two floors in the brightly colored interior are impregnated with the smell of paper, and enthusiasts of writing and drawing can be sure of finding something with which to indulge their pastimes.* ■ **La Formiga d'Or (42)** Avinguda Portal de l'Àngel, 5 - 08002 ☎ 93 302 39 42 *Although this bookshop is thoroughly up-to-date in style, it is in fact over one hundred years old, and its mission has remained unchanged: to provide the book lovers of Barcelona with the great literary masterpieces.*

In the area

Although the commercial boom of the 19th century resulted in an explosion of small businesses, Barcelona has managed to maintain its many markets, focal points for a still-thriving neighborhood life, even in times when the expansion of the city has been at its most intense. These

➡ Where to shop

43   44

La Boqueria (43)
La Rambla, 91 - 08002 ☎ 93 318 25 84

Ⓜ *Liceu, Catalunya* **Food** 🕑 *Mon.–Sat. 9am–9pm* 🏮 🍷 🛍

Opened in 1840, on the site of a Carmelite convent, the Boqueria is indisputably the best market in Barcelona, and this is proved by the fact that all the city's big restaurants buy their produce here. In fact, every imaginable foodstuff is available here, from the most mundane to the most exotic. For over 150 years the Boqueria has been synonymous with quality, courtesy and efficiency. It is also worth visiting for its architectural merits, especially the iron cupola, added in 1914, and the spectacular Modernist-style entrance. Refreshment can be taken at the counter of the Pinocho bar, where the market vendors also take a quick break, or in the Gardunya restaurant, which obviously takes advantage of the ingredients on offer in the market itself.

markets play an active role in the everyday life of Barcelona's citizens.

Mercat de Sant Antoni (44)
Carrer Comte d'Urgell, 1 - 08011 ☎ 93 423 42 87 📠 93 454 57 46

Ⓜ *Sant Antoni* **Books, records, video-games and a range of collectors' items** 🕐 *Sun. 9am–2pm*

Sunday morning. The butchers, fishmongers and fruit and vegetable sellers of the old Mercat de Sant Antoni have pulled down their shutters, and the place is invaded by a throng of collectors. This iron-and-glass covered market resounds with the voices of enthusiasts of all kinds – fanatics for books, old magazines, religious images, postcards, records, cassettes, videos, stamps, coins, toy soldiers, games … – who come here to indulge their passions: to buy, sell or do a swap. This market is thus one of the few remaining places in Barcelona where it is still possible to enjoy the fun of bartering! Even if you are not a collector yourself, take a stroll under the arcades, to enjoy the spectacle and observe the lengths to which people will go to satisfy their obsessions …

Philately (45)
Plaça Reial - 08002

Every Sunday morning, half of the beautiful Plaça Reial is taken over by the stalls of a colorful market reserved for philatelists and coin collectors, and both amateurs and owners of specialist shops gather round Gaudí's fountain of the Three Graces to sell, buy and swap.

Not forgetting

■ **Antichità (46)** Carrer Escudellers, 58 - 08002 *Every Saturday afternoon, this little street market offers inveterate bargain-hunters the chance to sift through piles of old articles, and maybe find something worthwhile.*

■ **Los Encants Vells (47)** Plaça de Les Glòries Catalanes *Every Monday, Wednesday, Friday and Saturday, from 9am to 6pm, this big square is taken over by the flea market: fascinating bric-à-brac with goods of all kinds, both old and new, at interesting prices, although real bargains are pretty hard to find!*

In the area

The Passeig de Gràcia, a wonderful Modernist avenue flanked by elegant mansions and paved with stones designed by Gaudí, is Barcelona's main shopping street. The stores' sophisticated window displays do not belie the quality of the luxury items for sale within.

Where to shop

Loewe (48)
Passeig de Gràcia, 35 - 08007 ☎ 93 216 04 00 ➡ 93 487 07 11

Ⓜ *Passeig de Gràcia* **Ready-to-wear, fashion** 🕐 *Mon.–Sat. 9.30am–2pm, 4.30–8pm* ▣ ⑪ *(in the lobby of the Princesa Sofia hotel)*

Loewe is rightly considered the most international of Spanish fashion labels, and the classiest for leather wear. Since 1943 its headquarters have been on the ground floor of a famous Modernist building, the Casa Lleó Morera. The interior decoration is resolutely modern in style – white marble, carpeting and precious woods – but ties in perfectly with 150 years of tradition and luxury.

Bagués (49)
Passeig de Gràcia, 41 - 08007 ☎ 93 216 01 73

Ⓜ *Passeig de Gràcia* **Jewelry, watches** 🕐 *Mon.–Sat. 10am–1.30pm, 4.30–8.30pm* ▣ ⑪ *La Rambla, 105 - 08002*

This prestigious Catalan manufacturer of jewelry and watches, famous the whole world over, has established itself in one of the most celebrated Modernist buildings in Barcelona – the Casa Amatller – and this in turn provides the inspiration for the incomparable Bagués style.

Colmado Quílez (50)
Rambla de Catalunya, 63 - 08008 ☎ 93 215 23 56

Ⓜ *Passeig de Gràcia* **Food** 🕐 *Mon.–Sat. 9am–2pm, 4.30–8.30pm* ▣

This is without doubt the most famous food store in the city. In these days of large shopping malls, it is a pleasure to rediscover the atmosphere of an old grocery … The owner of the Colmado Quílez stubbornly resists the encroachment of modernity and proudly affirms the store's distinctive character. Behind a window display with barely an inch of spare space, the staff, wearing uniform striped shirts, greet customers with respect and professionalism.

Adolfo Domínguez (51)
Passeig de Gràcia, 32 - 08007 ☎ 93 487 41 70 ➡ 93 215 13 39

Ⓜ *Passeig de Gràcia* **Fashion** 🕐 *Mon.–Sat. 10am–2pm, 4.30–8.30pm* ▣ ⑪ *Passeig de Gràcia, 89 - 08008; Avinguda Diagonal, 490 - 08006; Carrer Pau Casals, 5 - 08021*

The doyen of practical and comfortable fashion since the 1980s, Adolfo Domínguez has succeeded in making his creations accessible to everyone.

Not forgetting

■ **Vitralls Valvanera (52)** Passeig de Gràcia, 55 - 08007 *Small shop tucked away in the 'Bulevard dels Antiquaris', a shopping arcade specializing in antiques. It stocks artworks made out of glass, stained-glass windows of varying shapes and colors, religious articles and lamps.* ■ **Items d'Ho (53)** Passeig de Gràcia, 53 - 08006 *The ideal spot for buying original gifts, and an excuse for strolling inside the Bulevar Rosa, a small shopping mall with a variety of boutiques.*

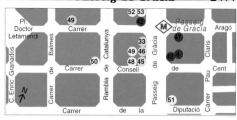

48

Loewe's sophisticated creations find the ideal showcase in this elegant shop in the passeig de Gràcia.

48

50

48

In the area
L'Eixample, a neighborhood designed on a grid system, with the *avingudes* and *carrers* spreading out like tentacles, lies mostly to the west of the Passeig de Gràcia. It is a sophisticated area, with some beautiful shops.

 # Where to shop

Altaïr (54)
Carrer Balmes, 69/71 - 08007 ☎ 93 454 29 66 ➡ 93 451 25 59

Ⓜ *Passeig de Gràcia* **Books** Ⓢ *Mon.–Sat. 10am–2pm, 4.30–8pm*

Dream of your next destination even while you are still on vacation: here is your chance, in this bookshop which specializes in tourism and would satisfy even the most globe-trotting spirits. Altaïr has information on every imaginable spot, even the most distant: in fact, there is an incomparable selection of tourist guides, road maps, city plans and out-of-the-way routes. And the choice of literature, anthropological studies and world music is in itself an invitation to pack your suitcase …

Bd Ediciones de diseño (55)
Carrer Mallorca, 291 - 08037 ☎ 93 458 69 09 ➡ 93 207 36 97

Ⓜ *Passeig de Gràcia* **Designer furniture** Ⓢ *Mon.–Sat. 10am–2pm, 4–8pm*

A shop? A museum? An art gallery? Bd Ediciones de diseño is more than anything the result of a gauntlet thrown down some twenty-five years ago by a group of Catalan architects and designers, including Oscar Tusquets, Pep Bonet and Lluis Clotet: to produce and commercialize, outside the usual networks, original furniture and household accessories which had never had the chance to be given shape before. Since then, the Bd team has realized historic projects by great masters like Antoni Gaudí, Salvador Dalí, Giuseppe Terragni, Mackintosh, Loos and Hoffmann, and produced works by contemporary artists such as Ettorre Sottsass, Álvaro Siza and Javier Mariscal. In 1979 Bd established its base in a Modernist building designed by Domènech i Montaner in 1895, the Casa Thomas, after helping restore it and saving it from dereliction. The result earned the architect Cristina Cirici, herself a member of Bd, the Spanish national prize for the restoration of historic buildings. This is just one of the many prizes which have marked the progress of Bd: such awards as the National Design Prize in 1989, and the European Community Design Prize the following year, underline the leading role it has played in international design and architecture over the last two decades. In short, a cultural shrine which should not be missed!

Planet Music (56)
Carrer Mallorca, 214 - 08007 ☎ 93 451 42 88 ➡ 93 451 70 78

Ⓜ *Passeig de Gràcia* **Records** Ⓢ *Mon.–Sat. 10am–9pm* 🚇 *Rbla. Catalunya 99 - 08008*

Since then the closure of the Virgin Megastore, Planet Music has become the most popular record store in Barcelona. Decorated by Alfredo Arribas, its stock, spread over 10,700 sq. ft, embraces records of classical music, pop, rock, jazz and soul, as well as a vast selection of music books and magazines.

Not forgetting
■ **Vasari (57)** Passeig de Gràcia, 73 - 08008 ☎ 93 215 15 15   Plaça Sant Gregori Taumaturg, 2 - 08021 *In this little shop on the Passeig de Gràcia, Vasari presents an original collection of jewelry, much of it inspired by neoclassicism.*

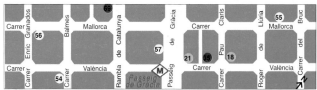

A section of the Passeig de Gràcia is devoted to record, book and designer shops including the famous Bd store.

In the area

You are about to leave Barcelona and you still haven't found all your gifts. No need to panic! Set off for the Passeig de Gràcia, lined with beautiful shops with enticing window displays. Here you will undoubtedly find a souvenir to take back to your family, or a more original present to

Where to shop

Gimeno (58)
Passeig de Gràcia, 101 - 08007 ☎ 93 237 20 78

🅜 Diagonal **Smoking accessories** 🕐 Mon.–Sat. 10am–1.30pm, 4.30–8.30pm

A peaceful haven for smokers, who are subject to such bitter criticism these days. On the outside, a large inscription on the beautiful window, framed in green wood, reads 'House of the Smoker', leaving no room for doubt: smokers are welcome here. The cozy interior, with its large, inviting armchairs, is reminiscent of an English club, and here even the most seasoned collector will be impressed by the incredible range of lighters, ashtrays, pipes and other articles …

Groc (59)
Rambla de Catalunya, 100 - 08008 ☎ 93 215 01 80 ➠ 93 487 16 19

🅜 Diagonal **Clothes and accessories** 🕐 Mon.–Sat. 10am–8.30pm ▭
🚻 Carrer Muntaner, 385 - 08021

If the specialist magazines are to be believed, the Catalan designer Antoni Miró is currently the darling of Spanish fashion, for both women and men. Miró also has a growing international reputation, as can be seen from the presence of his collections on European catwalks. Newcomers and connoisseurs all flock to the Groc shops to see his latest creations. The men's wear department in the basement also offers a made-to-measure tailoring service; the women's section includes, on the first floor, a collection of original silver jewelry, made exclusively for Miró by Chelo Sastre.

Vinçon (60)
Passeig de Gràcia, 96 - 08008 ☎ 93 215 60 50 ➠ 93 215 50 37

🅜 Diagonal **Household articles** 🕐 Mon.–Sat. 10am–2pm, 4.30–8.30pm ▭

It is impossible to miss this shop, housed in a Modernist building neighboring on Antoni Gaudí's famous Pedrera in a friendly and welcoming atmosphere, Vinçon displays some 10,000 different items over a total floor space of 32,000 sq. ft: all lovers of good design are certain to find something which will give a touch of originality to their home, be it a simple soap-holder or a voluptuous couch. Even if you do not want to buy anything, pay a visit to this winner of the 1996 Spanish Design Prize to discover the ideas of today's top designers and the newest trends.

Dos i una (61)
Carrer Rosselló, 275 - 08008 ☎ 93 217 70 32

🅜 Diagonal **Gifts** 🕐 Mon.–Sat. 10am–2pm, 4.30–8.30pm ▭

A glass-paneled automaton invites you to cross the threshold of this little shop. Its originality extends from its floor-tiles, a continuation of those of the sidewalk, to its stock – jewelry, watches, office materials … which is presented with great taste. The ideal spot for anybody in search of a gift which is out of the ordinary …

satisfy even your most demanding friends!

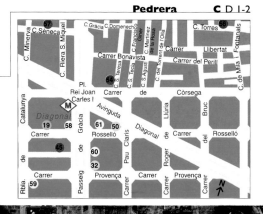

The Diagonal did not get its name in vain: this avenue dissects the city, diagonally … Its most elegant section, above the Passeig de Gràcia, is home to some of the most sophisticated shops in Barcelona.

Where to shop

Gonzalo Comella (62)
Vía Augusta, 2 - 08006 ☎ 93 237 96 73 ➠ 93 237 68 48

M *Diagonal* **Ready to wear clothes and accessories** 🕓 *Mon.–Sat. 9.30am–2pm, 4.30–8pm* ▣ 🚇 *Passeig de Gràcia, 6 - 08006; Capità Arenas, 3/5 - 08007; El Prat airport*

This chain, which sells designer clothes for men, women and children, has, over the course of more than a century, carved a place for itself in the history of the city. Ever since the Comella family opened its first shop in 1870, the customers have never ceased to flock to it … to such an extent that it now has nine shops in Barcelona and its outskirts (the most recent addition is in the shopping arcade in El Prat airport). All the Gonzalo Comella stores offer designer labels, from either Spain or beyond: Armand Basi, Pulligan, Miró, Genfins, Caramelo, Chipie, Liberto, Hugo Boss, Zegna. The same stamp of luxury characterizes the collection of top-class lingerie and accessories.

Pilma (63)
Avinguda Diagonal, 403 - 08008 ☎ 93 416 13 99 ➠ 93 217 90 77

M *Diagonal* **Designer furniture and furnishings** 🕓 *Mon.–Sat. 10am–2pm, 4.30–8.30pm* ▣ 🚇 *Carrer València, 1 - 08015*

A store recommended for those who appreciate good design, which offers a wide choice of original objects and unusual gifts. It is sometimes difficult to distinguish between the items for sale and the furnishings of the shop itself, which is spread over three floors, but the numerous sales people are always at hand to guide you through the details of the different sections …

Tapicerías Gancedo (64)
Rambla de Catalunya, 97 - 08008 ☎ 93 215 21 08 ➠ 93 215 88 17

M *Diagonal* **Wallpaper and furnishing fabrics** 🕓 *Mon.–Sat. 9.30am–1.30pm, 4.15–8pm* ▣ 🚇 *Carrer Bach, 9 - 08021*

A long tradition and high-quality products have made Gancedo an obligatory port of call for lovers of furnishing fabrics and wallpapers. The exceptionally wide selection has given this store a reputation which has long since crossed frontiers … so that interior designers and decorators from all over Europe come here to place orders.

Not forgetting

■ **Pertegaz Estudio (65)** Avinguda Diagonal, 423 2° 2ª - 08036 ☎ 93 209 59 22 ➠ 93 209 56 02 *Haute couture for men and women, with clothing made exclusively to measure. The prices and the image of the collection are only accessible to a select clientele. The establishment receives its customers by appointment only, and it does not have a ready-to-wear collection.*
■ **Rosa Bisbe (66)** Rambla de Catalunya, 121 - 08008 ☎ 93 217 41 39 ➠ 93 201 27 32 🚇 *Carrer Ganduxer, 20 - 08021; Avinguda Diagonal, 280 - 08018 This boutique is tucked away inside the Avenida arcade. The tiny space is given over to a beautiful selection of jewelry designed by Rosa Bisbe, who is currently very fashionable in Barcelona and has succeeded in carving a niche among the top names in her field.*

Established over a hundred years ago, Tapicerías Gancedo and Gonzalo Comella are Barcelona institutions.

Finding your way

The streets in Catalan
As all Barcelona's street names are now written in Catalan, it is a good idea to familiarize yourself with some of the most common terms you will come across in the city:

carrer *street*
plaça *square*
passeig *boulevard*
platja *beach*

rambla *avenue with central promenade*
avinguda *avenue*
passatge *passage*
ronda *ring road*

There are alternatives to the car ...

A rigorous organization of the city's traffic and a large number of parking lots (often with a charge) do not mean that you should automatically rule out public transport, which is very efficient and makes a superb complement to the tourist buses when you go sightseeing. The stops all have the additional advantages of a shelter and a small bench, so that waiting gives you a welcome chance to have a rest. All the information on public transport in the city can be found on the website www.tmb.net.

Barcelona is ...
Situated near the
2ⁿᵈ Western meridian
a little north of the
41ˢᵗ Northern parallel
and
393 miles from **Madrid**
687 miles from **Paris**
93 miles from **the French border**

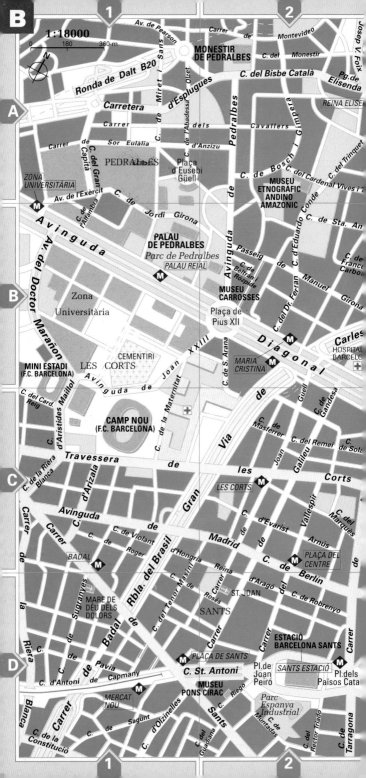

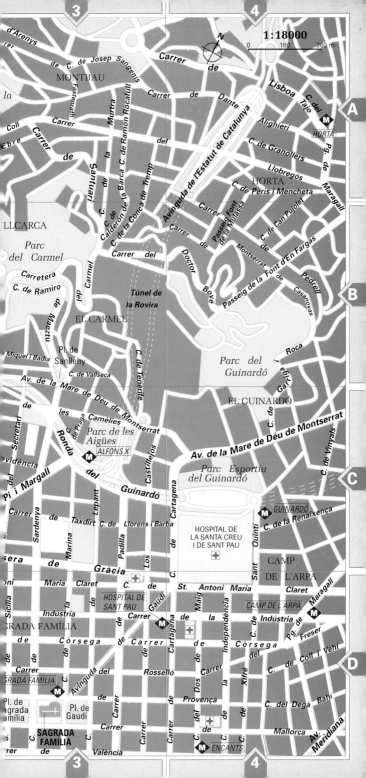

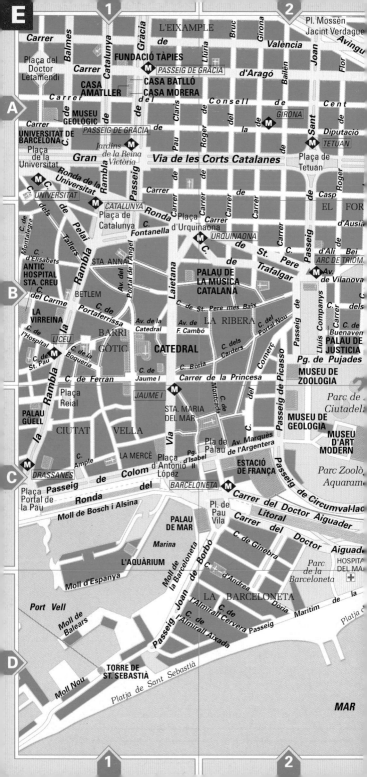

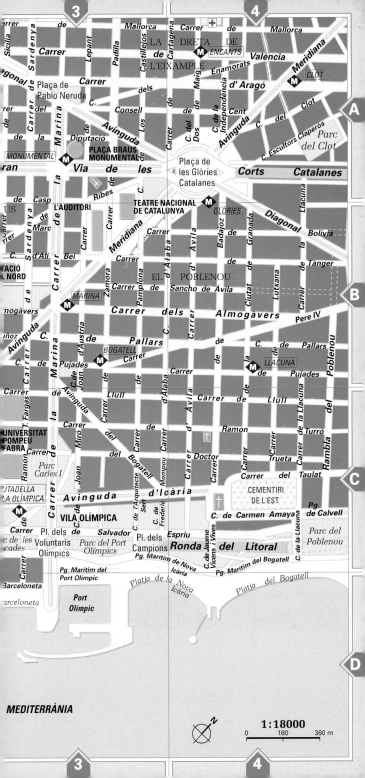

Subway map

er portar-te més lluny

Street index

Each street name is followed by a
bold letter indicating which map to
refer to, and a grid reference.

Index

All the practical information and useful telephone numbers concerning Barcelona and your arrival are presented in the section 'Getting there', pages 6 to 15.

General
Index

The Publisher would like to thank
The Spanish Tourist Office in Milan,
The Barcelona Tourist Office, the
TMB and Vilafranca del Penedès
Town Hall for their kind cooperation.

Picture
credits